ISBN 978-0-265-12219-8
PIBN 11061978

Contents

Vol. XXI.　　　　　　APRIL, 1909.　　　　　　No. 7.

ADVERTISING.

THE O. A. C. REVIEW is published by the Students of the Ontario Agricultural College, Guelph, Canada, monthly during the College year.

ANNUAL SUBSCRIPTION : Students $1,00. Ex-Students 50 cents. Single copies 15 cents. Advertising rates on application.

THE O.A.C. REVIEW

THE DIGNITY OF A CALLING IS ITS UTILITY.

VOL. XXI.　　　　　APRIL, 1909.　　　　　No. 7

Athletics in Canada and the Colleges' Relation Thereto.

BY GEORGE J. FISHER, M. D.,

Secretary Physical Training Department of the International Committee of the Young Men's Chirstian Association. Secretary Young Men's Christian Association Athletic League of Canada.

CANADA is an athletic nation. Her climate is particularly favorable to the development of splendid winter sports. What a beautiful sight to witness the snow shoe clubs tramping across the snow clad hills, or the toboggans speeding down their precipitous sides. One catches his breath as the daring ski-er leaps high into the air and clears a yawning chasm or a road upon the mountain side. What merry laughter, what wholesome fun, what abounding enthusiasm characterizes the skating parties, the cross-country runners and the boys upon the hockey courts. All through Canada the chromatic hues of toques, sweaters and cloaks against the snowfield of white produce a pleasing effect upon the eye. Then, too, the tang and thrill of quickened blood, the wind-kissed cheeks, the sparkling eye all give vigor and vitality to the participants.

This opportunity for healthful recreation is one of Canada's great assets. It provides the opportunity for the development of strong bodies, tense muscles and large hearts and vigorous lungs. These games produce hale and hearty young men and women. They are a great social factor, they add good cheer and wholesome social relations. They allow for national expression. Canada's winter sports reveal her national traits just as gymnastics reveal the stolid German characteristics or Gaelic football the Irishman's impetuous nature.

Canada's sports should be conserved. They should be honorably administered and carefully safeguarded. Every Canadian patriot should fight to the last to keep them from being commercialized, of letting other motives than sport for sport's sake creep in.

Sport should be socialized, not specialized. Every one should have a playground and every one should be a player. That type of athletic sports should prevail in which health is the

The College has been, in North Am ary and incidental.

But already the mercenary sport pro moter is trying to get his hands upon the sports of Canada, and use them for personal gain. Already so-called ath letic clubs are offering young men— and often boys in their teens—"induce ments" of money and special privi leges to play on their star teams. Some larger athletic organizations depend upon their gate receipts from hockey and other games to pay expenses. Already some athletes with ability are asking "what is there in it for me to play?" Let us remember Greece and Rome, when in their sports, the ideals which charac- terized their athletes in the days of their supremacy, and made her great, were later forgotten.

Canada's sports are her treasure. They should be kept pure and whole some. Canada's games are character builders, they must be conserved. The best men in the Dominion, the most influential agencies in the land should seek to make and keep them whole some, amateur, democratic. They should be for the participation of the many, not for the exploitation of the few. Their aim should be to make men, ruddy-hued, clean-limbed, well knit, muscle-toned men, not for the development of skilled athletes whose motive is the prize or whose aim is mercenary—though there is a place for honest athletic competition.

This effort for clean amateur sport is on. The crisis is upon us. Shall Canada's competitive sports be ama teur? The Colleges should help to set tle the problem. It is exceedingly worth while. In fact, viewed from the standpoint of its effect upon young men it is imperative.

The College has been, in North Am erica, the leading factor in athletics. Here teams have set the type of sports and the spirit which governs in them. Unfortunately, they have not always been pure and amateur. The contrary is only too true with many. But the reaction has come. Strict eligibility rules are being established, freshmen frequently are ineligible to participate on representative teams, a scholarship standing is required and competition is limited to three years. Faculties are interesting themselves and are tak ing a hand in the administration of college athletics. All these are helping greatly to purify sport and make them truly amateur.

But the College is too local in its operation. It is too exclusive in its relations. It has in the past been too self-centered, concerned only in its own athletics irrespective of the inter est of sport at large; as it affects the community or the nation.

The influence of the Colleges is need ed in the play life of the nation and they should join their efforts for the common welfare. Some time ago the Young Men's Christian Associations of Canada, by uniting together, and en tering the old Canadian Amateur Union, in company with other agen cies, rejuvenated and energized that latent agency, and made it a potent force for amateur sport, which it had not been heretofore. Some of the athletic clubs unfortunately wanted to employ athletes on a salary so as to get skilled ones, and withdrew from the reform body. While it caused divi sion, it separated the purely amateur organization from the so-called semi professionals. This had its good effect in drawing a sharp line between the organizations that stood for strictly amateur sport and those that did not.

The new Canadian Amateur Athle tic Union immediately flourished, and to-day is the most vigorous, and most purely amateur organization that has ever existed in Canada. It is growing stronger each day, and is constantly adding to its constituency the best ath letic elements in the Dominion. The Canadian Amateur Athletic Union is a sort of federation of all amateur bodies, rather than an autocratic organ ization that seeks to dictate athletic policies, and this is the most reasonable form of athletic administration.

Unfortunately, through misunder standing, the Amateur Athletic Union of the United States severed its alli ance with the Canadian Amateur Athle tic Union.

In the meantime the athletic clubs favoring the use of the paid athlete on the same teams with the amateurs, formed an organization known as the Federation. Strange to say this body was received into an alliance with the Amateur Athletic Union of the United States. In making this alliance, how ever, it presented a very interesting amateur statement. This refers only to its track and field sports and basket ball. Indeed the Federation was will

ing to agree to an amateur proposition from an athletic body outside of Cana da, which it refused to make with a truly Canadian body, and strange to re cord, showed anti-Canadian loyalty in the Olympic games of London. How ever, we believe, that even the friends of the Federation were not sympathetic with this attitude.

Now, where are the Colleges in this struggle for clean sport? Theirs is largely an attitude of neutrality. Some disregard both organizations. Some support the Canadian A. A. U., a few play Federation teams. The Colleges and Universities should, because of a strong national spirit, thrust them selves into the game and help to score results. The Canadian A. A. U., to gether with the Colleges and Universi ties of the Dominion can, if they are in terested in conserving what is best in Canada's sports, and purging what is bad, bring about those conditions where the play life and athletic sports throughout the land will make for health and physical power, will develop skill and make for character and truly exalt the nation.

These are the conditions in Canada's athletics. What shall be the Colleges' relation thereto?

IN THE SPRING FIELDS.

I tread the uplands where the wind's foot-falls,
Stir leaves in gusty hollows, autumn's arms,
Seaward the river's shining breast expands,
High in the windy pines a lone crow calls,
And far below, some patient ploughman turns
His great black furrow over steaming lands.
—*Wilfrid Campbell.*

The Swimmin' Hole on the Farm

BY G. H. CORSAN.

PEOPLE who work hard all day should have a reasonable amount of fun and relaxation. The non recognition of this has driven thousands of farmers' sons and daughters to the city.

If a stream run through your farm, be it ever so small, keep it clear and free from refuse of every kind, then select in it a favorable spot, and enlarge it so that it can be used for the purpose of swimming. A good swim after a hard day's work in the hay field is more refreshing than a sleep. But do not confine the privilege to the men and boys; encourage the women and girls to engage in the sport. They who have their farms bordering on a swift flowing river are fortunate, for there is no better fun than to run up the grassy bank for a distance, then to dive in and swim down with the current. To the average person unacquainted with the art, the vast possibilities of swimming and diving are not even thought of. For instance from a low spring board sixteen different dives, or head first entries into the

water can be performed, and in a full exhibition I demonstrate thirty methods of swimming.

One of the great drawbacks to swimmers, is the oft-attempted broad stroke-on-the-breast, as an elementary stroke. Instead of this I would advise the beginner to secure a pair of water wings, place them about the middle of the abdomen, then work the arms in a manner similar to that of a person paddling a canoe with a double-bladed paddle. The arms should work alternately, while the feet thrash the water like the strike of a fish's tail. The illustration shows the crawl stroke, with the swimmer's head in the water, but this position as a rule is adopted for racing purposes only, and it is not at all necessary that the beginner immerse his head. Also note that the body is in a horizontal position, for this is very essential to fast, easy swimming. By lowering the head and filling the lungs with air, the feet will rise, and thus the body will be driven through the smallest possible displacement of water. The crawl stroke orig

CRAWL STROKE.

The left arm, which is out of sight, is supposed to be pushing the water back, while the right arm is reaching forward to be dipped into the water. Notice that the legs are never bent at the thigh, but at the knees only. Also note the position of the ankles, the feet always pointed like a ballet dancer's. Breathe in through the mouth, snap the feet together.

CRAWL STROKE.

On account of a freak of the camera, the length of the arm is exaggerated, but this clearly shows the position of the wrist in gripping the water. Place the hand in the water gently, and then use the force in push ing back the water. The left hand has just left water with a kick which swings the arm forward, and saves the work of lifting it forward. Breathe out here through the nose when under water.

inated in Australia, and is one of the healthiest forms of exercise known. As a means of strengthening the lungs, and straightening the shoulders and spine it has few equals.

It is essential also if one is to reap the greatest possible benefit from this exercise, that he pay attention to the time he takes his accustomed plunge, and to the temperature of the water he is entering. Swim always before rather than after meals, and never bathe in water that is cold, as it has a decidedly weakening effect. Water that is comfortably warm is the best, for then one can stay in long enough to accomplish something really profitable.

Many of the drownings that are attributed to cramps, are simply caused through the inability of the swimmer to breathe properly when in the water, and this important phase of the art of swimming, can be learned only by careful and consistent practice. Should a non-swimmer be suddenly thrown into the water, or should he wade beyond his depth, dog-paddle to safety instead of throwing the hands out of the water, and making no attempt whatever to keep afloat. This can be done, and has to my positive knowledge saved the lives of many persons who had never before learned to swim. The common practice of bathers, when in trouble, to shout all the air out of the lungs, and to struggle wildly is a dangerous one, and many accidents could be averted if those who get into difficulties would just keep cool and at least make the endeavor to swim. The wisest plan though is to learn to swim now, then

CRAWL STROKE.

The hands push the water back and should not go too deep. The feet snap together. Note position of thumb and little finger of the hand that is in the water; thumb is always down, and little finger up; keep the hand similar to the blade of an oar always. Breathe out here through the nose. Let the beginner use only the arms at first, supported by wings.

you will be prepared for difficulties when they do arise. If shallow water is convenient learn to keep afloat there first, then venture to the deeper places; if you have only a deep pond at your disposal use the water wings, and you will be surprised to see how quickly you improve. Learn to be a swimmer somehow or somewhere, for it is not only one of the most enjoyable forms of sport to be found, but it is an accomplishment that no one can afford to be without.

THE CRAWL ON THE BACK.

Alternate overarm on back. Right arm recovering out of water, left arm pushing the water back. The legs give a short scissors kick with each arm stroke. Hook the wrists and reach the hands far back on entering the water. Do not slap the hands in, but dip in and then put on the pace.

The Awakening of China

BY G. H. UNWIN.

IN order to appreciate what the awakening of China means, we must review the situation in which that great empire—once the proudest in the world—finds herself to-day. For some years past the European powers have looked upon China, in her enfeebled and handicapped condition, as their private and peculiar play ground, in which they have indulged, so to speak, in a kind of international tug-of-war, the prizes being portions of territory, trading rights and conces sions which have been disputed, fought for and wrangled over with a fine dis regard for the lawful proprietors. Long and loud have been the discus sions, the reproaches and recrimina tions between the contending parties; but to China herself—the householder whose mansion has been so ruthlessly broken into, the proprietor whose gar dens have been trampled and dese crated—no consideration whatever has been shown. Her feeble attempts to make her claims heard have been ignored; her timid suggestions that she, and she alone, has the right to dispose of her own territories, have been met with derisive contempt; and she has been forced, not once but many times, to eat the bitter bread of humiliation, until in her very shame, she finds the courage to turn and as sert herself. For it is impossible to believe that a nation of such ancient and mighty traditions will forever tamely submit to the dictates of every aggressive "foreign devil" who may desire a share of her rich territories. "A worm will turn," and he who reads

the signs can have no doubt but that China has already commenced the "turning process; only, in this case, the worm has assumed the proportions of the largest of pythons, and the turn ing is likely to be fraught with danger ous consequences; for China, awak ened from her long sleep, China, con scious of new strength and a vast fund of reserve power, is a force to be reckoned with; and it is scarcely prob able that she will look with the kind est of feelings upon those, who, in the time of her weakness, trampled her in the dust and heaped the ashes of humiliation upon her head.

Let us consider, for a brief moment, the character of the Chinaman in order to see whether he possesses the qual ities essential to national greatness, whether he is worthy of more consider ation than has been shown him in the past. Unfortunately we are but poor ly informed with regard to the native of China. We know him only through the porcelain on our tables, with its lawless perspective, through the tea chest with its marvellous and incom prehensible hieroglyphics; at best we are familiar only with the lowest type of his nation; and hence we have but a degraded and incorrect view of a country, where the virtues of honesty, filial piety and politeness have been for centuries the basis of all moral and social upbringing, where the doctrines of Confucius, a man of blameless and absolutely unselfish life, are held in as great reverence as the Bible among Christians, as the Koran among Mo hammedans. It is only those men who have lived in the midst of the Chinese, who have been the recipients of those little courtesies of life which seem so trivial, but which mean so much, it is only these men, the missionaries, merchants and engineers, and the various European officials of the Imperial customs, who can have any true idea of the character of the native of China; and these men are unanimous as to his industry, his shrewdness, his determination and his exceptional honesty. In our mixed colonies in the Far East it is the Chinese who are the commercial backbone of the communities, who are the most loyal to their foreign associates, and the most amenable to government discipline. Are the tenets handed down from generation to generation, the reverence of parents, the obedience to superiors, the lofty ideals of literature and art, the sacred obligations of friendship so carefully instilled, the teachings of emperors and sages, are all these to be supposed never to have borne fruit? And because the view of life taken by a native of China differs at first sight from our own, are we to consider him as lacking utterly in all those qualities which go to the making of a man and a gentleman? Some years ago the Chinese were guilty of the un paralleled offence of calling the representatives of the proudest and most supercilious of civilizations, "outside barbarians." This was, of course, an unpardonable calumny; but such a weakness is excusable when we remember that at the time when our ancestors were naked savages, without arts, letters or written speech, China rejoiced in an ancient, complicated and refined civilization—was rich, populous and enlightened—had invented gunpowder, printing, the mariner's compass and the sages' "Rule of Life"; and had

grappled vigorously with that same problem of existence which Emmerson found as insolvable in modern times as it was then.

Recent struggles in the Far East have rudely shaken from their lethargy the Chinese, hitherto a nation of scholars rather than warriors. Close upon the heels of the "Boxer" uprising, which witnessed that unspeakable horror, a foreign occupation of the Sacred City, came the struggle between the mighty armies of the Bear and the Rising Sun, during which China was forced to stand aside, an agitated spectator of the despoiling of her territories, unable to lift a finger to protect them. Here was a state of affairs to make even the most bucolic of her subjects pause and consider whether a government which permitted such things were worthy of the name! And when Japan forced the great Russian Bear to his knees, then every Chinaman knew that, without speedy reform, his country was doomed. It was Japanese success, rather than European aggression that first aroused China to a sense of her duty to herself; for China has never loved Japan, formerly despised her, and now fears her. Hence it comes that, having taken a leaf out of her enemy's book and realizing that, in order to endure, it is necessary to progress, she is steadily and constantly Westernizing herself. Militarism is predominant; education has been revolutionized, and China is learning from her own enemies, how to fight them with their own weapons.

It is perhaps hard to believe that these four hundred millions of people, wrapped for untold ages in the mists of superstition, cradled in the bosom of ignorant conservatism, should suddenly, and to such good purpose, set about the work of their own reform; but the chance introduction of steam and electricity has made possible what years of bitter experience seemed unable to accomplish. Those provinces which have been hitherto separated by the barrier of distance from the heart of the Empire, are now being drawn closer and bound tógether by the iron bands of telegraph and railway. Those famous old viceroys, who turned themselves into miniature emperors, who formed an "imperium sub imperio," and defied the emperor's decrees, are now powerless in the grasp of a central power; and where formerly flourished the many-headed monster, Anarchy, a determined and long-armed government now distributes justice to the furthest boundaries of the Empire. Small wonder, then, that we hear of Chinese graduates in the great colleges of Europe and America; small wonder that far-seeing governments are hastening to proffer friendship, to obtain a place in the councils of the Empire. Great and powerful as Japan has become, China will be yet greater, for hers is a nation of thinkers and her great men can rank with the great men of the world.

The reality of the progressive movement cannot for a moment be doubted. For the first time, in the history of the Empire, the central authority has been enabled to enforce its decrees; for the first time the Provinces are activly and whole-heartedly engaged in furthering the Imperial policy, in anticipating the Imperial pleasure; China is beginning to "think imperially." She is knitting her disintegrated Provinces with iron rails and electric voices; she is extending the hand of friendship to modern education and religious freedom, and she is building up her army and navy on the most approved European models. What a vast field, what limitless possibilities seem to open up before a nation like this; an extent of a million and a half square miles, sheltering over four hundred millions of industrious people, producing and consuming three staples of food and clothing, wheat, rice and cotton—and three staples of luxury and comfort, silk, hemp and tea. When we mentally review this picture, when we think of China's myriads of toiling people, her unequalled area of fruitfulness, her vast resources hitherto practically "untapped," we can dimly conceive the effect on the balance of the world when this great force, hitherto inert and dormant, shall thrust its bulk into the delicately adjusted mechanism of our international and commercial system. One nation, exceeding in population the whole continent of Europe, comprising one-third of the population of the entire globe, composed moreover of people who have shown themselves the industrial equals of any upon earth, united by one common bond of nationality, the servants of one common emperor, and acuated by one common impulse, to raise their country to the front rank among the nations. Were we possessed of the magic carpet, and able to fly into the future and there, from some lofty, solitary pinnacle, review the world and all the nations of the world, what should we see? On the one side the nations of the West, powerful, proud, but isolated in their jealousy, each suspicious of her neighbour, each working for her own ends. On the other China, an awakened, electrified China, strong, alert, united, her people unweakened by internecine strife and international jealousy, sum moning her multitudes to the great battle for supremacy. Then will be the time for the white nations, if they would keep their place, to put aside their bickerings and selfish intrigues, and, joining in one common bond of brotherhood, make head against the menace of the Yellow Man. Let skeptics say what they will, let them stigmatize such prophecies—if a process of reasonable deduction can be called a prophecy—as visionary nonsense. It is this very attitude of serene confidence in his own security that constitutes the greatest danger to the White Man. We are apt to forget, we, the strong ones of the earth, that the term of another may come; hitherto we have shown to the Oriental only our "seamy side," our greed and avarice; arrogant in our strength we have displayed ourselves to him as violent, taking with the strong hand, trampling the weak. Can we blame him for calling us barbarians? In any case we should remember that he is a man like ourselves, capable of human achievements and human emotions. In the words of Kipling, the man of many sides, we find a key to the situation:

"Oh, east is east and west is west, and
    never the twain shall meet
Till earth and sky stand presently at
    God's great judgment seat,
But there is neither east nor west,
    border, nor breed, nor birth,
When two strong men stand face to
    face, tho' they come from the
    ends of the earth."

What matter what color he be, black, yellow, white? What matter under what sky he was born, what tongue he speaks? He's a strong man and worthy the respect of strong and weak alike all the world over. Let us learn to be on our guard against him as a possible foe, even to understand him as a possible friend. We must not, and indeed we cannot despise him.

Farm Management

BY PROFESSOR SPILLMAN, U. S. DEPARTMENT OF AGRICULTURE.

The readers of the O. A. C. Review may be interested to know something of the work done in the office of Farm Management in the U. S. Department of Agriculture. So many of the agricultural colleges of this country go to Guelph to get teachers that, I have no doubt that a good many of your students will, in the future, be co-workers with us in the States. This is all the more reason why they would be interested in our work.

The Office of Farm Management resulted from the recognition of the fact which forced itself more and more upon us—that the farmers of this country have, in the main, worked out the principles involved in farm practice and that the better class of farmers, even sometimes without recognizing the fact, really have uncovered fundamental principles relating to the successful conduct of the farm which would be of great value to others if they could be made common property. The early work of the Office of Farm Management was therefore the study of farm practice, and this is still the leading feature of our work. We divide the country up into districts and place one man in each district, whose duty it is to ascertain what types of farming prevail, which of these types are most successful, what effect they have on the fertility of the land and on the standard of living and their relation to markets, labor supply, capital required, etc. Especial attention is paid to the crops which thrive best under different conditions in a district, and to the methods used by the most successful farmers who are following each of the types of farming which seem to be best adapted to the region.

Most of the bulletins we have thus far published are merely descriptions of a few of the best farms we have found. These bulletins do not give a general idea of our work. It is as if we were developing a gold mine, and had not yet gone far enough to outline the pay streaks, but in our prospecting we have found a lot of fine nuggets, which have been carefully described. We are getting now nearly to the point where we are ready to show the public where the pay streaks lie. That is, we shall soon be publishing a series of bulletins that will give the results of our more general studies.

We are getting from some fifty farms a detailed account of every quarter hour's work done upon them. We are making careful surveys of these farms, and are plotting the fields, and are getting a detailed statement of their equipment and the capital involved in the various phases of this equipment, including the land, buildings, fences, implements, live stock, etc. From such data we hope to be able to work out the cost of all kinds of farm operations, the cost of producing crops, of handling live stock, and to ascertain what the profits are. Such facts will be exceedingly useful in planning the work of the farm.

Perhaps, I may in future numbers of The Review be able to give your readers some idea of some of the best farms we have discovered, and, perhaps, some more general ideas of farming in this country.

[Editorial Note.—Our request to Prof. M. Cumming, Principal of the Nova Scotia College of Agriculture, for a contribution to our columns, found him too busy to prepare an article especially for the Review. We publish below, his letter in which he speaks of the progress of his work in Nova Scotia, and to which he appends an extract from a report he is issuing, which we believe will be of interest to our readers.]

Mr. Editor:

You have asked me to contribute something to the columns of "The Review." My interest in the College at Guelph and its official publication, "The O. A. C. Review," prompts me to comply with your request. No paper which comes to my office is read with greater interest than the "Review," and I am pleased to note that in every way the editors are maintaining the high standard which has been set for this publication.

Our College at Truro is making splendid progress. Four years ago we commenced with an attendance at our regular course of seventeen; now we have enrolled forty-eight. Then we had at our short course sixty-eight, and at our 1909 short course we had a regularly enrolled attendance of 221, with an intermittent attendance of over 300. These figures in regard to the College may, I think, be taken as representing the general spirit of progress which is now manifest among the farmers of the Maritime Provinces.

As you are probably aware, the farmers of these provinces have, through diversity of employment, limited their farming operations, the same man at different seasons of the year being sometimes a farmer, a fisherman, a lumberman, or it may be, a miner. Hence, things agricultural have not progressed as they might have. Gradually, however, a new spirit, has been coming over the farmers of the Maritime Provinces, and a greater confidence in farming as a means of making a livlihood has been established. We, at the College, are endeavoring to our utmost to encourage this most desirable movement toward up-to-date farming. Progress is our word and building on the solid foundation which we had so strongly impressed upon us when studying at Guelph, we are endeavoring to enforce the fact that "In livestock lies the salvation of Maritime agriculture." This month we are issuing a report, bearing on the live stock industry of the province in which we state our confidence in the cow as a means through which our farms shall be emancipated. In this we have tried to pen a brief tribute to her and we submit it to you under the title of—

A Nova Scotian's Tribute to the Cow.

We have sung of a man and his achievements—of the poet, the orator, the statesman, and those who, in their lot in life, have done their duty. We have sung of our country—its resources, its beauties, its grandeur. We have written of the throngs of the city and have idolized the life 'midst green fields and by running waters. We have thrilled at the song of the bird and the speed of the swift limbed horse. We have wondered at the instinct of the beasts of the forest, the field, and the air. These things terrestrial have filled our minds. But who, that has pictured the brute creation, the noble horse, the mighty lion, or the songful bird, has stopped to think of her, who of all man's animal friends, is the greatest—the cow.

Remove her from this globe and think what we will take. Old England's roasts of beef, the food of her valor and solid achievement, those smoking steaks—we'll take them. That mug of milk by yonder high chair—we'll snatch it from the eager hands of that rosy-cheeked child. That plate of yellow butter, that pot of cream, that cheese—we'll take them and leave you to give thanks over dry bread and tea and strawberries unmellowed by these toothsome products of the cow. Those boots and shoes that save you from the snow and rain—we'll take them. And more too, for stop to think of what we owe the cow. From her head to her tail, there is not a thing but is used to minister to man's wants. Our milk, our cream, our butter, our cheese, all come from the cow. Her flesh is the food of all nations.

Her skin is on our feet and with it we guide our swiftest horse. We comb our hair with her horns. The very buttons that hold our clothes together are hers. We purify our sugar with her blood. We wash our hands with her fat. Her hair holds the plaster of our walls. Her hoofs are the source of our glue. Her bones and her blood fertilize our land. Her sons have drawn our plows and have cleared the fields by our settlers' cabins. None other like the cow. From morn to night, and from night to morn, she gathers her food and, even while we sleep, changes it into the food as well of our babes as of our aged parents.

Think of the commerce that would cease with her. Think of the long freight trains, the mighty ocean boats, the great stock yards, the creameries, and the factories all over the globe. Let her cease and half the world's commerce is at an end. Think of a Denmark, scarce two-thirds the size of Nova Scotia, exporting, through the medium of the cow, one hundred million dollars worth of produce. Think of a Holland vieing this. Think of what she might do for this province by the sea.

Grand and noble brute—of all man's friends the best. Where'er enthroned prosperity rules. We pay our tribute to you. And he that would abuse you, would fail to care for you and feed you as he ought, we would remove from his table all that you have placed upon it. We would exalt you in our province. We would plead your rights, for in doing so we plead for everybody; the smiling babe, the loving mother, the aged grandparent, the merchant and the laborer, the pauper and the millionaire—yes, for humanity itself.

Personal Reminiscences

BY RICHARD GIBSON.

THOUGH it was not my fortune to have met Bakewell, he was without doubt the greatest improver of live stock that Britain ever possessed. I was born within a few miles of Dishley; reared on a farm reeking with evidences of the former occupant —a member of the Bakewell Club— and the very soil was saturated with the memory of Bakewell.

The ordinary sheep of the country were ill-feeders, scraggy, maturing at three years, and not much better than the range sheep to be found at the Stock Yards in Chicago. Yet Bakewell within his lifetime regenerated these nondescript rent losers into hoggets that at one year old, if fat, were almost useless for the table. They, however, put the guinea stamp upon every Long Wool sheep in Britain. Lincolns especially were benefitted and the breeders thereof are to be congratulated, that while they retained the volume of wool they recognized the necessity of earlier maturity. Nowhere can such a display of mutton sheep be found as at Lincoln April Fair, some 25,000 hoggets in their fleeces, just over one year—such a sight can never be seen elsewhere, and Bakewell did it. Do we not read that four Lincoln breeders paid $5,000 for one Bakewell ram? Henry Dudding's father was one of the quartet. We cannot dwell, but we must not leave this unique personage without mention of his work with other stock than sheep. The Long-horns owe much to him. Their popularity has survived longest in the neighborhood of Dishley, where occasional herds may be found at the present time. Then the Shire horse, what we have to-day has been built upon the foundation laid by him; with Yorkshire swine his work is ever present. The personality of the man was distant and secretive. His works remain and while I cannot claim knowledge of the man I can recollect some of his apostles.

I must leave Bakewell and get to Robert and Charles Collings who were students of Bakewell's methods, improvers of the Shorthorn, while not originators like Bakewell. Their A. B. C. had been provided. They simply took up the task as left to them by the earlier worker. They availed themselves of the material supplied to their hands. The roung clay model was provided, all they had to do was to put the master's hand upon the clay and then polish. What our breeders have been doing up to date is simply perpetuating what has been. Here might be mentioned the names of earlier workers but all students can easily supply the same.

After Bakewell the line of thought led to Collings. Mason must not be forgotten, for he was a candidate for honors that were competed for by Bates and Booth. He was a true disciple of Bakewell for he liked his cattle to be fat as the Dishley Leicesters—as one of England's breeders pronounced them "carrying fool's fat"— hence from Mason follows Captain Barclay, who bought at Mason's sale, and there is not a Scottish herd to-day but what is saturated with Barclay blood, the earliest and most pronounced Scottish breeder until Cruikshank Brothers used the best at their hands, wise men, but not inspired breeders, they were wise enough to secure what was at hand for them and use it to best advantage. But oh, those "neeps" and the intelligent way in which the herds were managed. No better feeders or better feed can be found than in Aberdeen.

Before leaving Shorthorns, and I know nothing else, I admire other breeds like them, and acknowledge their usefulness, but I cannot bend the knee and worship them. Sir Charles Knightly must not be passed by. He absolutely ran his own herd to his own satisfaction, ignoring both Booth and Bates. What he wanted he was able to buy. He would insist upon milk as the main adjunct of his cows. With the milk instinct came the feminine face, fore quarter and the swinging milk vessel. But what dairy cows they were. To illustrate my appreciation, the first Shorthorn I ever bought in England for my own use was a Knightly Garland. As a landlord, as a genial companion, with his hunting friends, his name will never be forgotten.

We must leave the Shorthorns, though the subject is only approached, and away to the Sussex Down. What Bakewell was to the Long Wool sheep, John Ellman, of Glynnde, was to the medium wooled sheep. His work, like

that of Bakewell, was the regeneration of the sheep of his native downs, which as a result of breeding for generations from ill-grown, mis-allianced parents had become so inferior that none but an enthusiast would have undertaken the work. It was attempted; it was consummated in the one man's lifetime, with the aid of the Duke of Richmond. (for reference see Arthur Young's "Annals of Agriculture").

While Bakewell was a "clam" with few friends, John Ellman was a power in the land besides his sheep worship. He was recognized as a pioneer in sheep husbandry, but that is another matter requiring other investigation.

But, while Bakewell was basking in his selfish mood Jonas Webb was welcoming the crowned monarchs of Europe, no show place was so often visited or so great a welcome extended. While Bates was weighing his butter, Jonas Webb was entertaining potentates. My feeling goes out to him for did I ever spend more week ends than at Henry Webb's? Nor did I ever meet a more charming family; nor could any stranger get more near like home than Mrs. Webb's kindly reception; and then to the Village Church for the weekly service makes one of those red-letter days in one's life never to be forgotten.

I can write no more for the reason that I cannot personally record the history of Herefords or Angus cattle, nor of Hamps or Oxfords.

[Editor's Note.—All undergraduates of the O. A. C. are required to conduct original investigation work. This work is usually performed during the summer of the Junior Year. The results and summaries of which are printed in thesis form, bound and submitted to a committee for examination. After examination the theses are placed on file for future reference. The following are summaries of a few theses submitted in 1909.]

Investigations re. Concentrated Feeding Stuffs

THE composition of any feeding stuff is of interest to all intelli gent feeders of farm animals, for as long as the live stock industry is of paramount importance, so long must the question of feeding farm animals be the next in significance. This means that the farmer should know more about the relative value of foods in order not only to feed them intelli gently, but to estimate their value up on the market. At the present time the prices asked for cattle foods in Canada bear little relation to their ac tual food value. Foods are retailed at so much per ton, regardless of their composition or suitability to supple ment the ordinary farm foods.

In the United States where breakfast foods are more largely used and the by products sold as cattle foods, under nu merous and often meaningless names, the government has been compelled to give the matter serious consideration. As a result some of the states most affected have passed laws known as the Feeding-Stuff laws, whereby all manu facturers are required to secure a license, and provide a guarantee as to the per cent. of protein, fat carbohy drate and fiber, and to state specific ally what the component parts of the feeds are. With the ever-increasing population in Canada the demand for breakfast foods will undoubtedly grow, as well as the demand for concentrated foods for animals. It is generally un derstood that foods sold by cereal man ufacturers are of little value, being very low in food value, high in fibre, and of little use for feeding stock. Un doubtedly in a great many cases this is true. It is quite apparent to the. aver age reader that oat-hulls, for instance, as a concentrated food, would be of little use even for a maintenance ra tion, yet oat-hulls can be used very ad vantageously to give bulk to a food such as cotton-seed meal. In this con nection we must also remember, that there are many by-products of a very high feeding value. For example, in the manufacture of starch from corn, we have what is known as gluten meal. This is often as high as 25 per cent.

in protein, and is used to a large extent by cereal mills to raise the nutritive value of their foods. This being true, it does not seem unreasonable to sup pose that by intelligent use of these different by-products, that foods could be mixed suitable for almost any class of stock.

The writer carried on a series of di gestive experiments with four com pound foods, viz.: Molac Dairy Feed, Schumacher Feed, Banner Cattle Feed and Victor C. & O. Feed, in order to estimate their relative value upon the basis of digestibility.

The following table includes the chemical analysis and digestive coeffi cients of the four feeds in ques tion.

Sample.	Protein.	Fat.	Carbohydrates.	Fibre.	Ash.
Molac D. F. 14.87		4.68	56.65	11.01	5.36
% Digested........ 80.70		94.60	81.28	57.17	54.59
Schumacher S. F.... 12.31		2.64	59.55	9.76	3.08
% Digested........ 81.48		85.6	79.9	39.34	33.77
Banner C. F........ 11.38		2.11	65.37	7.23	2.37
% Digested........ 77.75		77.16	77.2	77.17	77.4
Victor C. & O...... 9.910		1.78	61.02	10.71	3.48
% Digested........ 57.78		71.74	75.68	35.88	42.0

In examining the above table we find that the first three feeds compare very favorably with oats, in composi tion. Molac is somewhat higher in pro tein, this being due undoubtedly to the addition of cotton-seed meal. The fat content has been raised in the same way. It is generally noticed in study ing foods that those high in fibre are proportionately low in digestibility. This, however, does not always prove true, especially when a number of the ingredients which make up one food and one of the number happens to be a highly digestible nutrient, such as

cotton-seed, or gluten meal. This is clearly demonstrated in the above table where Molac, although possessing the highest fibre content, nevertheless shows a greater digestibility than the other foods under consideration.

Owing to the fact that Molac and Schumacher are used largely as dairy foods, and that the others are more general purpose foods, it will simplify matters, if they are compared under these heads.

From the above table we find under the head of protein, that Molac posses ses 14.78 per cent. of which 80.70 per cent. is digestible. Schumacher Feed contains 12.31 per cent. protein, 81.48 per cent. digestible. Calculating from these figures, Molac possesses 240 pounds of digestible protein in a ton, whereas Schumacher shows 206 pounds, a difference of 34 pounds per ton in favor of Molac. In considering the other two feeds we find that Banner possesses 11.35 per cent. protein, as compared to 9.91 per cent in Victor; of this 77.25 per cent. is digestible in Banner, and only 57.25 per cent. in Victor. This gives in one ton of each food 175.8 pounds prtein for Banner, and 114.5 pounds for Victor, a differ ence of 61.3 pounds in favor of Banner. It will be seen at a glance that Banner exceeds Victor in all desirable consti tuents, being higher in both total and and digestible content. Space will not permit a further discussion of the table, but this should be sufficient for the reader to understand the table and study it for himself.

It can readily be seen from the fore going data that there is quite a differ ence in composition between these four feeds, and shows the necessity of feeders knowing something of the rela tive value of foods of this nature before buying them to supplant the ordinary farm foods, or as an addition to a ra tion. Even our most common foods— wheat bran for example—has become so adulterated that many feeders have stopped using it. Not many years ago wheat bran contained about 13 per cent. digestive protein, while to-day

it is not unusual to find it as low as 10 per cent. In the writer's opinion it is high time for the farmer to have pro tection in this matter. It is under stood that a committee has been formed to petition the government re garding laws governing the sale of mill foods. This is a move in the right di rection, and should receive the support of every intelligent feeder of stock.

C. F. Bailey.

Part II.

In connection with the above article a brief note might be added concerning two of the feeds therein mentioned, viz.: Molac and Schumacher.

During the winter of 1907 a prac tical feed test was made of these foods, by the writer, to ascertain their value as compared with bran and oats for milk and butter production.

The test was run for three months. It was made with six cows, two from each of the three breeds represented in the College herd, being Holstein, Jersey and Ayrshire.

The cows were fed a definite and constant amount of roughage, consist ing of clover and timothy hay, silage and roots. Both feed and milk was carefully weighed and an accurate ac count of each kept.

The following tables give in brief the results as obtained, estimating the amount of grain required to produce one hundred pounds of milk and fat.

Experiment No. 1.

Molac versus Oats, mixed with bran.

Ration.	Total lbs. of Grain	Total lbs. of milk.	Total lbs. of fat.	Grain for 100 lbs. of milk.	Grain for 100 lbs. of fat.
Bran and Molac	350	1,347	49.674	25.98	704.5
Bran and Oats	392	1,350	49.4	29.37	793.
Gain of B. and M.	42	3	.274	3.39	88.5

In consulting the preceding table we see that Molac proved somewhat su perior to Oats when mixed with bran. The amount of bran fed in both cases was the same. We note that there was 42 pounds more of the oats fed than of the Molac. The Molac pro duced three pounds less milk, but .274

lbs more fat. While it took 3.39 lbs. less to produce 100 lbs. of milk and 88.5 less for 100 lbs. of fat.

Experiment No. 2.

Oats versus Schumacker, mixed with bran.

Weekly average, 3 cows.

Ration.	Total lbs. of Grain.	Total lbs. of milk.	Total lbs. of fat.	Grain for 100 lbs. of milk.	Grain for 100 lbs. of fat.
Bran and Schumacher	182	743.3	23.755	24.4	766.3
Bran and Oats	203	763.5	26.927	26.58	886.4
Gain B. and S........	21	20.2	3.172	2.19	120.1

About the same comment can be made on this table as on the preceding one. The amount of bran in both ra tions was equal. The total amount of milk and fat was less from Schu macher, but the amount for 100 lbs. of each was less.

Experiment No. 3.

Molac versus Bran, mixed with Oats.

Weekly average, 3 cows.

Ration.	Total lbs. of Grain.	Total lbs. of milk.	Total lbs. of fat.	Grain for 100 lbs. milk	Grain for 100 lbs. fat.
Oats and Molac.......	168	544.3	20.53	30.86	818.3
Oats and Bran.......	189	544.75	20.83	34.7	907.3
	21	.45	.3	3.84	98.0

In the above table Molac makes a very good showing compared with Bran, when mixed with Oats. There was equal weight of Oats in each ration.

Experiment No. 4.

Molac and Schumacher versus bran and Oats.

Weekly average, 6. cows.

Ration.	Total lbs. of Grain.	Total lbs. milk.	Total lbs. fat.	Grain for 100 lbs. milk.	Grain for 100 lbs. fat.
Bran and Oats.......	392	1193.3	44.3935	32.85	883.0
Molac and Schumacher	392	1179.	44.392	33.25	885.3
Gain B. and O........		14.3	.0015	.60	2.3

In the above rations equal weights of Molac and Bran were used and also equal weights of Oats and Schumach er. It might be expected from the re sults of the foregoing experiments that Molac and Schumacher would prove superior to the Bran and Oats, but such is not the case, although the two rations are almost equal. As the table indicates Bran and Oats produced 14.3 lbs. more milk, and practically the same amount of fat. There is only a little over one-half pound difference in the amount it took for 100 lbs. milk and only 2.3 lbs. difference grain for 100 lbs. fat, but what there is favors Bran and Oats.

This would almost go to show that although Molac and Schumacher mix well with Bran or Oats, they are not any better than Bran and Oats when mixed together, yet compare very favorably with them.

With this data in view we may conclude by saying that as long as these foods are sold at a reasonable price and consistently mixed they will prove to be a very profitable way of disposing of much of the by-products of our cereal mills.   P. H. Moore.

The Ash Constituents of Oats

The mineral substances which enter into the composition of plants constitute the ash or that portion which remains after all that will burn has passed away. These ash constituents, though slight in amount, stand in a peculiar and interesting relation to the life processes and living structures of plants. They have received less attention in the past than their importance deserves. Their functions are so complicated and important as to constitute a wonderfully interesting field for investigation by the scientific agriculturist. This is a field in which the chemist, the agronomist, the physiologist and the average farmer find a common ground of interest for these ash forming substances, constituting the ash of plants, come from the soil,

through the plant and thence to the animal.

The mineral substances of food stuffs are present in four conditions, in solution in the plant juices, as crystals in the tissues, as incrustations in cells and in chemical combination with the living substance.

The ash content of any species of plant varies considerably as affected by the character of the soil, the manuring, the season, the date of maturity, and the variety grown. The varieties in the following analysis were grown under similar and natural conditions. Hence, we may assume, to some extent at least, that the factor, variety, does exert an influence in the composition of oats.

Mineral Elements in the Ash of the Oat Grain.

VARIETY	Per cent Ash	In one hundred parts of pure ash.									
		Silica SiO_2	Iron Fe_2O_3	Lime CaO	Magnesia MgO	Phosacid P_2O_5	Potash K_2O	Sulphuric acid SO_3	Soda Na_2O	Manganese Mn_3O_4	Chlorine Cl
Liberty	3.27	34.22	1.14	3.53	7.24	24.21	20.92	2.98	2.21	1.24	.09
Siberian	2.72	35.99	1.72	3.07	2.28	26.57	20.05	2.82	2.66	.80	.04
Joanette	2.76	29.81	1.92	3.46	5.06	28.90	22.60	3.90	1.92	1.02	.41

Mineral Elements in the Ash of Oat Straw.

VARIETY.	Per cent ash	Silica. Si O2	Iron Fe2 O3	Lime Ca O	Magnesia Mg O	Phos. acid P2 O5	Sulph. acid So3	Potash K2O	Soda Na 2O	Manganese Mn3o4	Chlorine Cl
Liberty ..5.17		45.32	.97	8.43	3.40	4.73	3.80	26.31	3.77	1.22	1.05
Siberian ..5.58		38.02	1.32	8.92	2.74	6.12	6.43	28.88	2.98	.39	1.86
Joanette ..6.82		42.60	1.55	8.74	3.67	3.04	5.40	27.22	3.50	.40	1.88

In one hundred parts of pure ash.

Some definite knowledge of the character and distribution of the ash constituents in the grain and straw of oats is revealed in the above tables. The straws of these three varieties contained, in each instance, a higher percentage of ash than was found in the grains. Another marked difference existing between the ash of the two parts of the crop is noticed in the fact that the mineral matter held within the grain is a more constant quality.

The compounds of phosphorous, potassium and calcium are prominent in the composition of the oat plant. These three elements, besides being important constituents, are quite as important plant foods, and therefore demand very prominent consideration.

From the above tables the ash of the oat grain is thus seen to be composed largely of silica, potash and phosphoric acid, while silica, potash and calcium form the bulk of the mineral matter of leaves and stem.

The percentage of K_2O in the straw exceeds in each case that found in the grain. However, the results show that it is quite evenly distributed throughout the oat plant. A point of not a little importance is brought out

in the above figures in that potassium occurs in the entire plant in the largest proportion of any of the essential ash elements.

We notice that a very large percentage of the phosphoric acid removed from the soil in a crop of oats is found within the grain. It is apparent from these figures that nearly the whole of the P_2O_5 of the plant had been accumulated within the seeds at the time of ripening. Phosphorous is one of the two essential ash materials which was found to be present in larger quantities in the grain than in the straw, at the time of maturity.

The percentage of calcium is much higher in the straw than in the grain. This element does not accumulate in the seeds to such a great extent, as for example P_2O_5. Only about one quarter of the total quantity of lime removed in a crop of oats is in the grain.

These analyses show that as between different varieties of the same kind of plant the ash content and its composition varies quite widely. Variety, is then, one of the factors which influences the variation in composition of vegetable materials.

N. Foster.

Horticulture

The Outlook for Apple Growing in the East

BY B. S. PICKETT, M. S., PROFESSOR OF HORTICULTURE, NEW HAMPSHIRE
COLLEGE, U. S.

IN TWO PARTS—PART I.

APPLE growing in the North East ern United States, and in Can ada is a much discussed indus try at the present time. It seems prob able that to-day is a transition period in the history of the apple industry in this section of North America. Will intensive methods of apple culture re place the haphazard methods so long productive of but low average profits? Will spraying become the rule and not the exception in the East? Will the box package replace the barrel? Must we find cheaper gift packages than bar rels or boxes or must some method of returning or disposing of such pack ages be devised? Will the East ever supply as fancy a fruit trade as the far West, or must Eastern apples become merely a standard for cooking, evapor ating and cider stock, while the far West grows our dessert fruit? Pro vided the East fails to produce so fancy an apple as the far West, will the ad vantage of proximity to market and ex port points more than compensate for the difference in quality of fruit? Will apple growing in the East pass out of the hands of farmers into those of spe cialists who will rent farm orchards, plant and grow large commercial orchards, establish cold storage houses, and generally take over the business of apple production and marketing? Will co-operative apple growers' and shippers' as sociations save the situation or help solve the problem of successful apple growing in the East? These are ques tions and conditions that confront the student of the apple situation in the North Eastern United States, and in Ontario, Quebec and the Maratime Provinces in Canada.

The factors which make for the pro fitable culture of any crop are, of course, the determinants of the outlook for that particular branch of agricul ture. The questions which are cited in the previous paragraph are answerable, pro and con, according as the business of apple growing in the East conforms or fails to conform to certain basic principles. If the factors which in fluence the apple producing business in the East are correctly determined and duly valued, the question of the profit ableness of the industry and the man ner of conducting it can be answered; and the whole matter can be settled with mathematical nicety.

But the factors that make for the profitable culture of no crop can be determined with absolute accuracy.

THE DEMAND IS GOOD.

Therefore, it is necessary for every in dividual to study his own conditions, and situations, with the utmost earnest ness and foresight, if he is to determine with approximate correctness the ulti mate success of a venture in commer cial apple growing. In this article the writer has endeavored to analyze some of the conditions which prevail in the Eastern apple growing sections, to in dicate the possibilities of the industry, and to some extent point out the direc tion of its line of development.

Among the factors of prime import ance in apple growing are suitable con ditions of climate and soil. Are the conditions of soil and climate in the New England States, Ontario and the Maritime Provinces of Canada favor able for apple culture? Let the experi ence of two hundred years and of thou sands of successful orchards in every section of these regions be a clinching argument. Count the number of suc cesful apple nurseries in operation in these districts and compare them with other states and provinces. Compare the total and average production of On tario, Nova Scotia or the New Eng

land States with similar areas else where, and you will be convinced that however, much their prestige in the apple-realm may have fallen in the world of print, there is nothing in the market reports to give one a pessimis tic outlook on. Eastern apple orchard ing. The region under discussion offers the widest possible range of soils and possesses every variety of slope and exposure favorable for specific pur poses or varieties. It possesses a suffi cient yearly rainfall to make irrigation unnecessary, on the whole has remark ably favorable blossoming periods, and has a wide choice of cleared land suit able for apple growing at prices much more reasonable than are demanded for orcharding lands in the far West.

Of equal importance with suitable soil and climate in successful commer cial apple growing is a suitable market. Without the latter the most excellent soils and climates in the world will not be sufficient to bring profitable returns from the orchard. Are the markets open to New England, Ontario, and the Maritime Provinces able to take at good prices enough first-class apples to compensate the growers of these re gions? The conditions in Canada are somewhat different from the conditions in the New England States, though both have points in common. The Bri tish export market is open to both, an ever growing market capable at all times of taking care at paying prices of every first-class apple that either country may send. The possibilities of the apple market in Great Britain have never been realized. The mother land takes only a moiety of the fruit which it will take when every British town and city has been organized to use and taught to rely on the American supply of apples. The continent of

Apples form the standard filling for pies. Apple pies made by students of the Macdonald Institute are particularly recommended.

Europe is slowly but surely becoming a customer for our apples, and the export trade will expand more and more rapidly in that direction as the years go on. Ontario and the Maritime Provinces have open to them a fair, though not a remarkable, home market. New England is rich in an urban population capable of using unlimited quantities of apples. Here is the opportunity to organize special trades, to supply private customers, to save expensive transportation charges and car refrigeration. Here is an opportunity to develop growing, specialized marketing, and a high type of fancy apples.

To the writer's way of thinking, the market outlook for the apples of Ontario, Nova Scotia, and New England is dependent on the growers and not on the consumers. The demand is good. The prices are almost always remunerative, and often they are exceptionally so. During the present winter first-class Baldwins have sold

in the Boston market throughout the months of January and February for six dollars per barrel. Ordinary sound Baldwins of good cooking quality have not brought less than three dollars per barrel. Twice during the month of January the writer was unable to buy Northern Spy on the Boston market at any price.

Every standard variety of apple has been proportionately high this winter. The demand at the moment of writing is not nearly equalled by the supply; and, while this condition does not obtain every year, a careful study of the trade for several successive years shows a fairly constant and relatively high price from December to March, in all our leading home and foreign markets. Even during the season of 1907-1908, when the dealers lost heavily on the apple speculations, the prices obtained for stored fruits were sufficiently high to have netted handsome profits to all parties in a normal year, and the growers received prices higher perhaps than were ever obtained before.

There is less fluctuation in the ac tual demand for apples than one might suppose. The many uses to which this fruit is put are factors that steady the call for apples. It has come to be a sign of a true farmer to want ap ple sauce two or three times a day throughout the season. Apples are the standard filling for pies. Baked apples are upon the menu cards of every res taurant and café worthy the name in Canada or the Northern United States. Apple butter, apple cider, apple vine gar, and dried apples are standard pro ducts of the crop which forms our sub ject. All these products are being used in greater quantities every year. One of the accompanying illustrations shows a dining-table centerpiece in which apples take their place with oranges and grapes for decorative pur poses.

Now-a-days the successful market

ing of perishable products is frequently dependant on transportation and stor age facilities. Is the region under con sideration well equipped in these re spects? Certainly the East is nearer the export markets than the West. In lower freights it has always an advant age of first importance. In respect to quick marketing of perishable varie ties, it must necessarily have an even greater advantage, for besides the sav ing effected in time by nearness to market there is a large sav ing in cost of packing, in waste of slightly over-mature but immediately marketable fruit, and in icing charges. In special cases the Eastern grower may ship by express, whereas the West erner must, on account of the exces sive cost of this means of transporta tion, rely wholly on the slower freight service. In faster freight schedules and number of trains the preponderat ing advantage is in favor of the East. The accommodations rendered by the eastern railroads leave much to be de

APPLES TAKE THEIR PLACE WITH ORANGES AND GRAPES FOR FANCY TABLE DECORATIONS.

GROWN IN THE EAST ON YELLOW TRANSPARENT TREE, SET FIVE YEARS.

sired, but unquestionably they are as yet superior to those offered in the West.

Our storage facilities are not ideal. Nevertheless we are better furnished with these than are most of our neighbors and competitors. Ontario has been particularly energetic in the erection of storage houses. New York State growers long ago learned the advantage of winter storing of apples and practiced it to such an extent that the dealers in our large city markets rely largely upon New York apples during the months of February and March. The New England States have not developed the home storage idea to any appreciable extent, but the growers here use the commercial plants of the city freely. No other apple region offers the same opportunities for cheap storage. The two natural refrigerants, cold air and ice, furnish cheap means of preservation. Wood, perhaps the cheapest and most effective constructive insulating material, is lower in price here than in any other apple growing region except the Pacific Coast, where artificial refrigeration must be resorted to. The problems of refrigeration in transit are being earnestly worked upon and will be duly solved. In view of these facts, therefore, the writer sees no reason why the East should view pessimistically the transportation or the storage factors in fruit growing.

THE O. A. C. REVIEW

EDITORIAL STAFF.

F. C. NUNNICK, '10, Editor.

S. H. GANDIER, '11, Associate Editor.

H. SIRETT, '09, Agricultural.	J. W. JONES, '09, Staff Photographer.
G. H. CUTLER, '09, Experimental.	G. H. UNWIN, '09, Artist.
A. G. TURNEY, '09, Horticultural.	MISS B. WILLIAMS, Macdonald.
O. C. WHITE, '10, Athletics.	MISS L. JULYAN, Assistant Macdonald.
S. KENNEDY, '10, Old Boys.	MISS E. M. WHITNEY, Locals.
C. M. LEARMONTH, '10, College Life.	P. E. LIGHT, '11, Locals.

C. F. BAILEY, '09, Business Manager.

Editorial

Athletic Number

It will be noticed that in this number of The Review considerable space is given to the different phases of Athletics. Our aim is to impress, if possible, upon a greater number of the students, the importance of developing oneself physically as well as mentally, a strong mind in a strong body is a good motto, and one to which we will do well to give more attention. To the men who leave these halls this spring to return next fall we would say keep in training, so that you may be strong and in the best of condition to enter the sports next fall. We have the material for a winning Rugby team if the men will but train. Each man can contribute his share towards making our team a winning one by keeping himself in good condition. Let every man who returns next fall be strong and ready to do his part in making Athletics a stronger feature here than ever before in the history of the College.

Disappearance of Magazines

We have on the ground floor of the College a large parlor beautifully furnished for the use of the students. Here they may spend a few spare hours very profitably reading the magazines which are placed there by the Literary Society and The Review. It is a regrettable fact, however, that the magazines and papers disappear so quickly after being placed upon the tables. If those dispicably selfish ones who persist in carrying away what does not belong to them, much to the inconvenience and loss of the rest of the student body, would take into consideration the fact that others have as much right to read these periodicals as those who carry them away, and would desist from this contemptible practice, it would be more in keeping with the spirit of fairness and fair play to all.

The periodicals which the Literary Society provides are wanted to be placed on file at the Library for reference, and if numbers are missing it breaks a volume and makes it incomplete and almost useless to those wishing to use it as a reference in time to come.

The magazines which The Review places on the tables are for the most part exchanges received from Colleges in Canada and in other countries. Many students enjoy reading other college papers, as many new ideas are obtained from them and we all like to see what is going on and how they do things in other Colleges.

For these reasons we ask that the students put forth every endeavor to prevent the carrying away of magazines from the college parlor, and from the Y. M. C. A. reading room, where they are wont to disappear in a similar manner.

Since the last number of The Review went to press the Athletic Association has been made the recipient of a **Another Donation** shield bearing the College Coat of Arms. This shield was made by G. D. Pringle, of Guelph, and presented to the Athletic Association by him. This is the first one made by Mr. Pringle, and for this reason we feel the more proud of it. It now adorns the college parlor and we desire to express our appreciation of the kindness shown us by Mr. Pringle who has already presented our Athletic Association with two cups.

Upon the entire student body rests the responsibility of electing officers for the majority of **Electing Good Men** our college organizations before the close of the spring term. We speak of it as a responsibility since it is largely upon the judgment of the students that the success of each society and association for the ensuing year depends. The majority of college men do not look upon the matter in this light, and many do not even consider it necessary to attend a meeting which has for its purpose the election of officers. If dissatisfaction is afterwards shown as to the men in whose hands has been placed the administration of the affairs of a certain society, it is generally the students who have taken no interest in the elections who evince it. In all justice to the various associations, to the officers, and to the students themselves, it is highly necessary that each student as far as possible should exercise his influence in choosing the best men to act upon the various executives and committees. Careless choice and careless voting is sometimes manifest, though happily in most instances the danger is overruled by the more level-headed majority. Too often men who have become popular through various achievements are nominated by their admirers for positions entirely unsuited to them. Some men are nominated because they are good fellows generally, execu tive ability scarcely being considered. Then there are those students who become overloaded with work of this nature. It is not uncommon to find a man holding two, three, or even more offices on different committees and executives. Such a man is generally a student of exceptional ability, and may be capable of accomplishing the work of each office satisfactorily, but too often he is almost forced to accept one or more of these appointments against his will. There appears to be a natural law that if a person is willing to assume a certain amount of responsibility, the more he finds himself called upon to undertake; but there is a limit for every human being in his capacity for work. It is not fair to overload individual students with responsibility of this nature, since often it necessitates undue neglect of very important work of the course. Therefore in electing officers for the executive boards of the various college associations, choose widely as well as wisely.

SPRING.

After long months of waiting, months of woe,
Months of withered age and sleep and death,
Months of bleak cerements of iced snow,
After dim shrunken days and long drawn nights
Of pallid storm and haunted northern lights;
Wakens the song, the bud, the brook, the thrill,
The glory of being and the petalled breath,
The never wakening of a magic will,
Of life restirring to its infinite deeps,
By wave and shore, and hooded mere and hill;
And I, too, blind and dumb, and filled with fear,
Life-gyved and frozen, like a prisoned thing,
Feel all this glory of the waking year,
And my heart, fluttering like a young bird's wing,
Doth tune itself in joyful guise to sing
The splendor and hope of all the splendid year,
The magic dream of spring.

—*Wilfrid Campbell.*

Oratorical

THE crowning event of the year in literary work was the eleventh Annual Oratorical Contest, held in the gymnasium on March the fifth. The Oratorical is always looked for ward to with keen interest and this year's contest was in every way a de cided success.

The College orchestra played several selections and relieved pleasantly the heavy strain resulting from continued attention to the speakers. The selec tions added much to the classical effect which is always felt at this literary evening.

There were five speakers, and every man did his best to win the coveted prize—a Standard Webster's Diction ary. The judges, Rev. W. H. Crews and Professor J. B. Reynolds, decided that the order of merit was as follows:

1, Mr. G. H. Unwin, who delivered the prize oration on "The Awakening of China," made a brilliant address. Mr. Unwin showed that he was a scholarly English student, possessing eloquence and mastery of the English language. (We would advise every one to read carefully Mr. Unwin's ora tion in this issue.)

2, Mr. A. McLaren spoke on "Rob

G. H. UNWIN,
Winner in Oratorical Contest.

bie Burns,' with patriotic enthusiasm, and although not very strong at the be ginning, he made an exceptionally strong finish.

3, Mr. J. M. Lewis handled his ora tion, "Education and Citizenship," in oratorical form, possessing the truest voice, and clearest enunciation. His style, however, was exaggerated ac cording to our standard of oratory.

4, Mr. W. M. Waddell. His subject, "Master Forces in National Progress," was ably handled, but he lacked some what the force and eloquence of the previous speakers.

5, Mr. A. McTaggart. His subject, "Imperial Federation," was forcibly de livered at first, but decreased markedly in strength towards the conclusion.

Several vocal solos were rendered by Miss Henderson, in a clear soprano voice, and the audience appreciated her singing by vigorous applause. Mr. C. M. Cassel also sang and the presenta tion of the dictionary concluded the evening's program.

Union Literary.

The second meeting of the Union Literary Society was held in Massey Hall, on February the twenty-seventh. An excellent program was provided, and the popularity of these meetings was shown by the crowded hall.

Miss Hartley rendered the opening number, a vocal solo, in her usual sweet, clear voice, and was heartily encored.

The address from President Creel man was the feature of the evening's program. Our President spoke on his recent trip to Europe, taking us through Scotland, Italy, Germany, and France, delighting the audience with his interesting and humorous remarks. Miss Kilpatrick rendered a classical

piano solo in a brilliant manner, bring ing forth merited applause. Mr. Staf ford's reading was enjoyed by every one, and he was called back a second time.

The debate, "Resolved that Canada should now bear a share of the finan cial burden of Imperial Defence," gave a large scope for strong argument.

Mr. R. McDonald, leader of the af firmative, representing the Maple Leaf Society, made a strong plea for the affirmative, but made the fatal mistake of speaking overtime. Mr. G. H. Cutler, leader of the negative, spoke excep tionally well, outlining forcibly Cana da's present position in relation to Imperial Defence.

Mr. A. McMillan, supporter of the affirmative, gave a carefully prepared speech, but lacked somewhat in force.

Mr. J. W. Jones delivered a snappy address, refuting several strong argu ments of the affirmative.

The judges decided in favor of the negative. The College orchestra rend ered delightful selections in the usual pleasing style. Mr. Sinha sang the Hindoo National Anthem, and trans lated the words into English.

The Barton-Hamer medal was pre sented by Professor G. E. Day, and he wished the recipient, Mr. N. D. Mac Kenzie, who stood *highest* in our team at Chicago, prosperity and success in his chosen line of work.

The critic's remarks by Rev. W. G. Wilson, were brief, but valuable, and the meeting closed by singing "God Save the King,"

Public Mock Parliament.

On February the twentieth, the hon orable members of the Legislature (students assuming parliamentary of fices) assembled in the gymnasium for a session.

The gymnasium was filled with an attentive audience, who expected to see legislators in action, and they were not disappointed. The Address from the Throne outlined the measures for consideration of the House. The ad dress was adopted and the House pro ceeded to business. According to the Opposition the Government did not have very much business, and many took the opportunity to enlighten the legislature on several interesting facts, both national and personal.

A bill respecting the taxation of bachelors was introduced, and several minor bills received a reading.

The Government endeavored to show their wisdom in framing such an important measure, and the Opposi tion endeavored to show that the usual graft and bribery were underlying the Government's proposals.

Now and then an Independent rose to his feet, and exclaimed his views. The wordy war waged on, even the Macdonaldites coming in for their share of the "rubs" from the efferves cent members, and only the call to "order" from the Speaker from time to time checked the flow of sesquipeda lian verbiage.

A vote was taken, and the bill re specting the taxation of benevolent bachelors was passed, owing to the easily swayed Independents voting with the Government.

An adjournment was moved and car ried, thereby bringing one of the most successful mock parliaments to an end.

Y. M. C. A.

The study of the lives of great and good men cannot result otherwise than in lasting benefit. The members of the Association enjoyed a literary treat on the evening of February the eigh teenth. President Creelman gave us a short, spicy and interesting address in his characteristic manner on "The Life and Times of Abraham Lincoln." He laid special stress on the manliness of Lincoln, and the obstacles which he had to overcome to reach the Presiden tial chair. In the course of his re marks he very forcibly impressed upon his hearers that it was a blessing to be born poor.

One week later J. A. Paterson, K. C., of Toronto, discussed the "Lay men's Missionary Movement." Un doubtedly this was the ablest mission address we have listened to in recent years. He explained its commence ment, the idea of the movement and drew conclusions as to its probable out come.

Frequent interspersals of humor and literary touches were very entertain ing, but the straightforwardness and sincerity of Mr. Paterson were convinc ing powers.

One hundred and twenty-five dollars were very willingly contributed by the boys to the Tokio Mission work.

Professor Reynolds spoke one even ing on the Niagara Conference Cam paign, dwelling upon the advantages of such a student gathering and urged all who could possibly make necessary arrangements to be present. Professor Reynolds conducted a Bible Class there last summer, and he knows ex actly what is to be obtained at this conference, held in June at Niagara-on the-Lake. The retaining of this confer ence on Canadian soil rests wholly with Canadian students. It is neces sary to be represented by a large num ber, and we desire that everyone should go, if it is possible. The Association will assist to a certain extent in de fraying expenses.

Junior "At Home."

The Assembly Hall in Macdonald Institute was the scene of an unique gathering on the evening of March the fifth. The Junior Conversat committee invited the girls on the Macdonald Conversat Committee, and the other members of the Junior Year to spend a social evening in remembrance of the pleasant Conversazione days.

After everybody had been introduced, all proceeded to make jolly, by amusement and general liveliness. Various "stunts" were performed much to the amazement of the "curious ones." The hypnotist succeeded in influencing several strong minds and puzzling problems were solved by esoteric methods. In spite of the fact that everything was apparently "straight," yet it was maintained by many that there was something "crooked."

Refreshments were served to the fifty present, and when they gathered to sing the parting song general regret was expressed—the time had gone all too quickly. The girls showed their appreciation by singing a touching refrain, and the boys heartily responded by giving their class yell.

STUDENTS GOING TO WORK.

Athletics

Varsity Swimmers Visit College

SATURDAY, March 6th, was the occasion of another big day in the history of the College swimming club, when Varsity's crack swimmers met the College boys in a of themselves, turning the tables on Varsity in more than one event. At that, though, Varsity came out on the long end of the deal, with a fair margin of points to their credit. In swim

O. A. COLLEGE SWIMMING TEAM, 1909.
First Row—Musson, Palmer, Cleverly, Bell-Irving, Keegan.
Second Row—Harries, M'g'r Water Polo; Marryat, Unwin, Pres. Swimming Club; Treherne, Ryan.

friendly contest. It will be remembered by our readers that College took part in the competition at Toronto in February, and met with rather indifferent success. On this occasion our boys gave a very much better account ming and plain diving there was not so much to choose between the two teams, but in fancy diving the visitors had it on our boys easily, and it was in the latter events that they made most of their gains.

Shortly after three o'clock Announc er McFayden called upon the contest ants in the "50 yards dash" to take their places. In the first heat Ryan represented College, and pitted against him was McKenzie. After giving a few instructions as to the methods he would use in starting the contestants, and a warning not to plunge till the pistol had been fired, Dr. Reed gave the word and away they went. Mc- Kenzie got off to a fine start with a lead of six feet, which Ryan could not quite overcome. In the second heat Shaw was just a little too fast for Treherne, and this also went to Varsity. The winner's time in both heats was 36 seconds. The "plunge for distance" went to College, after an interesting contest. Johnson appeared to be the winner until the last dive, when Harries snatched it from him in a great plunge of 47 ft. 7 in. In the "50 yards three styles," Ryan fully re deemed himself for his defeat in To ronto, winning a great race, his time being 41 2-5 seconds. McPhedren got second place in this event. In the "dives for form," Varsity took both first and second places. They attempt ed difficult dives and executed them with a degree of perfection that one does not often have the opportunity of seeing. Keith, Canada's finest gymn ast, won first place, with Corrie a good second. The "100 yards race" also went to the visitors, McKenzie win ning in 1 min. 25 2-5 sec. In the "tub race" Rogers and Powell, both of Col lege, again battled for supremacy. Powell led for a length and a half, but then met with difficulties, and Rogers triumphantly passed him and landed the race by a few feet. Follow ing this was the "50 yards back swim," which Varsity won in 47 seconds. The

last event, the "relay race," went to College on a foul that was just as un intentional as it was unlucky. Varsity had slightly the better team, and cer tainly were unfortunate to lose the race in the way they did.

The polo game which followed the swimming and diving competition was a fast one while it lasted. College started out on the aggressive, and after a few moments' play shot a goal, but it was disallowed by the referee. Varsity then took a hand in the game, and by some pretty combination work succeeded in notching the first. On the change of ends, College again be gan to press hard. They kept the ball almost entirely in their own hands, and rained shot after shot on Varsity's goal, but they either went wide or were blocked by the goal tender; at last Keegan secured the ball and by a pretty shot from close range, tied the score. The third quarter had just nicely opened when one of the Varsity players was seized with cramps, and as they had no one to replace him, and were pretty much exhausted by their heavy day's work, they decided to de fault. College was playing a strong game when it ended, and from a spec tator's point of view appeared to well merit the victory.

Inter-Year Polo.

Owing to the non-entry of the fourth year polo team to the inter-year series, the championship this year was left to be decided between the three junior years. This, however, did not in the least degree lessen the interest taken in the game, and it may well be said that the series was one of the best ever held at the College. A double schedule was played, and as the second year have gone through the season without a defeat they are the undis puted champions. They are perhaps one of the strongest teams representa tive of a single year that the College ever possessed. Every member of the team is a good swimmer, and they use splendid judgment in passing and shooting, which is just as essential a feature in water polo as in hockey or football. Altogether they are a well balanced team, and merit fully the dis tinction they have attained.

February 19th—First and second years played the opening game of the season, and as the score indicates it was a walkover for the Sophomores. They swam all around their oppon ents, piling up the huge score of nine teen goals, while the Freshies were un able to negotiate a single tally.

February 23rd.—The Freshmen met their second defeat, this time at the hands of the third year. They were not, however, so completely outclassed as in the previous game, but it was quite evident from the start that they could not win. Faulds easily handled their long shots, and nearly every at tempt they made to carry the ball close to the third year goal before shooting was broken up by Harries, whose well directed return shots kept the oppos ing goal tender guessing all the time. The score was 7—3.

March 1st.—The second year gave the Freshies another bad drubbing, the latter being saved from a whitewash by the narrow margin of one goal, while their conquerors rolled up an unlucky thirteen. There was nothing to it but that the second year were the better all-round team, and won as they pleased, although it may be said of the Freshmen that they showed im proved form from their first game, and need only practice to develop a first

rate polo team, for they have among their number many really good swim mers.

March 2nd.—The second year won from the third year by a score of 7—1. The Juniors were weakened by the absence of Bowman and Guillett, who were replaced by White and Moor house, both novices at the game, con sequently it was not as fast and close at it might otherwise have been. The Sophs. played a winning game all through, and only the fine work of Harries saved the Juniors from a worse defeat.

March 9th.—Third year again trim med the Freshmen, score 10—2. The Juniors were on the aggressive from start to finish and won handily.

The final game between third and second years went to second year by default.

The final standing of the teams was:

	Won.	Lost.
Second year	4	0
Third year	2	2
First year	0	4

Inter-Year Basketball.

The concluding games of the basket ball series did not bring forth any very close contests or unexpected results. The Seniors landed the championship winning all their games, while the other three teams tied for second place. The fourth year played superior ball all season, and quite outclassed any of the other teams, as the scores will show. The three junior years were about equal in strength, and it would be an interesting struggle if they were to play off the tie.

March 4th.—The second and fourth years met in a game that was all fourth year. For only a short period in the second half did the Sophomores have a look in. They opened the half very fast, and succeeded in shooting a couple of baskets in quick succession, but the Seniors then steadied down and won as they pleased, score 36—7.

February, 25th.—Third and first years played an interesting game, the honors going to the Juniors, by a score of 21—17. The third year secured a lead in the first half that stood them in good stead later on, for the Freshies got into the game in the second period, and made things warm around the Juniors' basket, so much so that they almost succeeded in evening up on

	Won.	Lost.
Fourth year 3		0
Third year 1		2
Second year 1		2
First year 1		2

Inter-Year Baseball.

By their dexterous wielding of the willow another championship falls to the lot of the Seniors. They succeeded in putting to naught their most dangerous opponents, the Sophomores and Juniors, and thus have gone through the season without a defeat. Coke pitched great ball this term,

THE TOSS-UP.

several occasions. The third year always managed to pull away however, and when the whistle blew they had four points to their advantage.

March 15th.—The Seniors had an easy time of it with their less experienced opponents, and trimmed the Juniors by 47—10. The Seniors passed well, and when they shot it usually resulted in a score, whereas the Juniors' combination was wild, and so closely were their forwards checked that they seldom got an opportunity to try for the basket.

This game finished the series and left the teams in the following order:

having much better control than he did last fall, and this together with the way the whole team slugged the sphere to all corners of the gym. accounts for their clean record of victories. The Sophs. gave them a scare in their game, but that was the extent of the harm done, and the Juniors died an easy death, by the wide margin method.

February 17th.—The Dairy boys made their second appearance in base ball uniform, losing the game by 19—4. The Sophomores did the trick easily, outplaying their opponents in nearly every branch of the game.

February 24th.—Third year van quished the Freshmen in a six-innings game. For the first two innings it looked as though the contest might be a close one, but after that the Juniors donned their batting clothes and simply ran away with the game.

March 1st.—The meeting of the fourth and second years proved to be the best, and most interesting game of the whole series. The fielding of the Sophs. was almost perfect, and just about counterbalanced the heavy hit ting of the Seniors. The fourth year

games ever pulled off here. The score was 20—18.

March 3rd.—The Juniors and the Dairy men hooked up for a game, in which the "lacteal fluid" experts were trimmed to the tune of 36—3. They couldn't connect with Nunnick's curves. while their pitcher was pum melled unmercifully, and their fielders made many costly errors.

March 8th.—The Freshmen and the Dairyites tried conclusions, and though science was somewhat lacking, the game was brimful of excitement

SLIDING HOME.

never had a great lead, but in the last three innings a single fluke might have meant the loss of the game to either side. Excitement was intense, and the players were nerved to the highest point, for the championship practically depended on the result. Both pitchers were cool, and the fielders never missed a chance. With two men on bases and two out, the Sophs. were just two runs behind, but the batter was caught at first and the last chance of winning lost. It was a fine exhibi tion of baseball, and will be remem bered as one of the best inter-year

for the supporters of the two teams. They were evenly matched, but the Freshmen had the luck, and won out 13—11.

March 10th.—The Juniors and Sen iors came together, and the Seniors demonstrated their worth by running off with the game in easy fashion, at the same time cinching the champion ship. They were at their best, batting and fielding in fine style, while the Juniors seemed to lack the vim that they showed in previous games, letting up when their opponents began to as sume the lead. The result was 29—15.

The remaining game between sec
ond and third years has no bearing on
the championship, but will decide
which of the said teams is to have the
honor of second place.

The standing of the teams is as fol
lows:

	Won.	Lost.	To play.
Fourth year 4	O	O	
Third year 2	I	I	
Second year 2	I	I	
First year I	3	O	
Dairy .... o	4	O	

Boxing and Wrestling Tournament.

The annual boxing and wrestling
tournament, held on Saturday, March
13th, provided an excellent afternoon's
entertainment for the students, and the
few visitors who gathered in the
gymnasium to witness our amateur
pugilists and grapplers perform. Some
good bouts were pulled off, and some
new material brought to light, both in
the boxing and wrestling.

There were just two classes in the,
boxing, under 145 lbs. and over 145
lbs. In the former class were entered
Whyte, Petch, Unwin, and Pillsworth,
and in the latter Beckett, Kelso, Fain
and Palmer. There were no knock
out blows, in fact hard hitting was not
indulged in to any great extent, most
of the boxers being content with jabs
to face and body that counted points,

but that did not inflict serious punish
ment.

The opening bout was between
Whyte and Pillsworth. Whyte had
all the science, and easily outpointed
his opponent. Petch and Unwin were
the next to clash and they furnished a
spectacular bout. Petch was speedy
and reached Unwin with long swings,
while Unwin could not very often con
nect with his more agile opponent. In
the final between Whyte and Petch,
Whyte showed excellent generalship;
he kept well out of reach of Petch's
swings, and led out only when he saw
a good opening. As a result of this
not many blows were struck, but the
majority were credited to Whyte. In
the heavyweight class Beckett easily
handled his smaller opponent Kelso,
and Palmer in his engagement with
Fain, broke his thumb and was forced
to retire at the end of the first round,
which was slightly in his favor.
Beckett in the deciding bout with Fain
won handily. He had the advantage
both in height and reach, and Fain
found it almost impossible to get in
on him.

The wrestling established new
champions in every class. Sorley cap
tured the 125 lb. class, and Fraser, in
the 135 lb., overcame Clark, last year's
champion, after three strenuous bouts.
Peart and Trethewey (145 lbs.) had a
hard tussle, but Trethewey was the
cleverer of the two, and in a mix up
while both were down, secured an arm

hold and gradually forced his oppon ent over. Miller, who competed last year, carried off the honors this year by throwing Baldwin in the finals of the 158 lb. class. There were but three entries in the heavyweight class, Moore house, Kennedy, and Beckett. In the first round Kennedy and Beckett came together. They were evenly matched and neither had a distinct advantage until Kennedy secured a body hold, and threw Beckett suddenly to the floor, on his shoulders, where he held him. In the deciding contest Moor house and Kennedy battled for several minutes before a fall was secured. Moorhouse was fresh, and strong, and had the better of the bout, although Kennedy squirmed out of many tight corners before both shoulders finally touched the mat.

Following is a list of the winners:

Boxing.

145 lbs. (under)—1, Whyte; 2, Petch; 3, Pillsworth.

145 lbs. (over)—1, Beckett; 2 Fain; 3, Kelso.

Wrestling.

125 lbs.—1, Sorley; 2, Davis.

135 lbs.—1, Fraser; 2, Clark; 3, Hutchinson.

145 lbs.—1, Tretheway; 2, Peart.

158 lbs.—1, Miller; 2, Baldwin; 3, Brown.

Heavy—1, Moorhouse; 2, Kennedy; 3, Beckett.

A Progressive Move.

The Athletic Association has for some time past been severely handi capped in its endeavors to raise ath letics to the high standard they should hold at an institution of magnitude such as ours. True we have pro gressed rapidly in the past, but when we compare our present state with that which we might have attained

had we but had the means to carry out many proposed plans, we must admit that we have failed to live up to the opportunities that were quite within our reach. Nothing in the way of im

RUGBY

provement can be done without money, and the lack of this is the im portant factor in college athletics that has so hampered the Athletic Executive in its efforts to improve up on existing conditions.

For many years the students have felt the need of, and have been call ing for a football coach; basket ballers have been making just demands that a team be placed in some league; base ballers have been clamoring with equal right, for a similar privilege; the lovers of soccer football feel that more attention to their line of sport is due them; a second hockey and foot ball team placed in a league would be very much in the interests of those games; the gymnasium is constantly needing additional apparatus; more of our representatives should be sent to compete in the various athletic meets held in Toronto and elsewhere, if we are to maintain our good standing among the colleges; in short the ex penditures that we should make are more than double the amount of our receipts.

After careful thought, and an inves tigation into the manner in which

HOCKEY

fee. A student body meeting was called, and when it was proposed that the constitution be changed, and that hereafter four dollars be the regular fee, there was a unanimous vote in favor of the proposal.

Such an attitude on the part of the students, is surely a sign that they have every confidence in our Athletic Executive, and that they are willing to stand by them to no mean extent, in their endeavors to achieve greater things than have been done in the past. It shows their truly loyal spirit towards athletics, and with such whole hearted support as the students are willing to give we may reasonably expect better things in the future.

other colleges dealt with such problems, the Executive decided that the only solution of the difficulty was to obtain from the students an increased

To What Extent Should a Student Enter Athletics?

BY J. H. CROCKER.

According to his physical and nervous makeup, the student may enter the realm of athletics, and there is no rule that will guide all, except that a man is to take that exercise in quality and quantity to be equivalent to a day's work. And a day's work will be enough of vigorous movements to cause that exchange of tissue so that nature will work out her own laws and bring to the student that feeling of well being and fitness which in itself gives balance and poise, a steadiness to the eye and strength to the muscle which united with an educated mind demands a purpose in the life. The student should not take athletics seriously, but should, like the English sporting man, enter for the sake of the game. The championships should

not be his class of sport, but rather that kind of game which has the most recreation in it for him without the mental and nervous strain which is bound to follow a hard game and incapacitate him for close study for several days.

And yet if we circumscribe a student with reference to his athletics there is a danger that we may rob him of just that bit of spice without which he would be willing to forego most of the games.

So it will resolve itself into a question of each man making a study of his own desires, and his own needs. Every man hopes to live that life which will count for most. Therefore to attain the greatest efficiency the student must be at his best in mental and physical fitness to grasp that knowledge which his opportunity is giving to him.

Most of the athletics now held un der college jurisdiction counts as a very important factor in the develop ment of character, and this coming to a man in his transition period surely is a part of his college work.

To play the game, to be one of a team that will meet an equal or greater force in an equal number of oppon ents, and yet by superior physical fitness, individual headwork, or better generalship, win a victory; is a test which in itself makes character, and without character there is no man hood.

There is therefore a place in the life of every student for some form of re creation and competitive athletic work properly supervised.

The kind of work each should adopt can only be decided after the student has consulted the Director of Physical Work, and has had a thorough examin ation. Then according to his age, his strength physically, and lastly and most important of all his nervous con dition with the advice of the Director, commence systematic athletic work to accomplish a three-fold purpose.

1st. To attain a place on a college team for its social and man-making qualities.

2nd. To work that he may be put to the test and develop a strong character.

3rd. That he may take the regular exercise which will keep him best fit ted to accomplish a year in study with out that loss of vitality which leaves so many men wrecks at the end of their college career.

Therefore let every student put sys tematic, recreative athletic exercise in some form into his college time table and make it a part of his college life,

and keep the time thus set apart in pro per bounds.

His time will be profitably spent. He will accomplish more from every stand point, and he will reach a higher point of efficiency in his public or private life, in business or in a professional career.

Any man that does not take exer cise must take time to be sick.

Be regular in your exercise.

Have stated periods for field or gym nasium work, and never miss it at those times.

Be interested in your work and en joy everything that you do.

Take a short vacation every day and use it for exercise.

Exercise will do for the body what the intellectual training will do for the mind.

Educate and strengthen it.

One especially good exercise is swimming; it brings all the muscles into play and afterwards there is a re laxation which means perfect rest.

Out of doors, deep breathing exer cise while walking is good; it will in crease the circumference of the chest.

Regular exercise followed by cold baths and simple diet will wonderfully help men to live clean lives.

Our Old Boys

Professor John A. Craig, of Texas, who has accepted the position of Director of the Oklahoma Experiment Station at Stillwater, is the originator of a system of live stock instruction by score card and actual judging of live stock in agricultural colleges. He is the author of "Judging Live Stock," and of many bulletins written when he was at the Wisconsin, Iowa and Texas Experiment Stations. He was instrumental in assisting Professor Henry, of Wisconsin, in establishing the first short course in agriculture. At Ames, Ia., he carried on with Professor Curtiss the first school in live stock judging which was the forerunner of corn judging schools. He has judged live stock at the leading state fairs and important expositions.

Professor Craig was born in Ontario, attended the Ontario Agricultural College at Guelph, completing a two-years' course. On graduation he became managing editor of the "Canadian Live Stock and Farm Journal," filling this position for three years. He was then engaged to fill the Chair of Animal Husbandry in the Wisconsin College of Agriculture, which he held seven years, when he resigned to become senior member of the firm of Craig & Stevenson, owners of a 1,350-acre farm in Wisconsin and breeders of Shorthorns and Shropshires. For three years he was Professor of Animal Husbandry and Vice-Director of the Iowa Experiment Station. He resigned to become editor of the "Iowa Home

stead." Later he became Director of the Texas Experiment Station and remained three years, when he purchased a small stock farm adjoining San Antonio, Tex., and has engaged in stock farming during the past two years.

Billy Munro, B. S. A., '06, who has been till the present time District Representative of the Ontario Department of Agriculture at Morrisburg, has resigned from his position to accept that of Manager of an Experimental Farm at Rosthern, Sask., under the Dominion Department of Agriculture. The principal line of work followed will be experimenting with fruits, to find out varieties suitable to the rigorous climate of the prairie provinces. Although the farm will be chiefly a fruit experiment station other work will by no means be neglected, as experiments with field crops will be carried on and we may predict that results will be obtained that will be of inestimable value to the farmers of Saskatchewan.

R. M. Winslow has accepted a position under the Horticultural branch of the Department of Agriculture of British Columbia, his duties commencing April 1st. "Windy" is a graduate in horticulture, and while at College became an ardent admirer of our sister province that lies beside the Pacific, and gives such promise of leadership in horticulture. We wish him every success, and trust that not for long will he tread alone the long and stormy path of life.

Previous to his acceptance of his pre sent position he represented the Depart ment of Agriculture at Picton, where he was very successful during the short time that he held his position. He will be succeeded at Picton by A. P. McVannel.

F. A. Clowes has been appointed as sistant to J. N. Hare, District Repre sentative at Whitby, and Reg. Duncan goes to assist Frank Hart at Galt, War ren resigning his position to return to the farm.

H. W. Scott, B. S. A., '07, has gone from the East to the West, from Farm ers' Institute work in Nova Scotia, to the Department of Agriculture of Al berta.

We were very glad to have with us again for a few days Mr. B. Barlow, and to know that he has entirely re covered from his severe illness. Mr. Barlow was Lecturer in Bacteriology at the College until his ill health neces sitated his resignation, which was tendered last spring.

Jas. D. Leitch, an associate of the class of '08' has left the hardware busi ness, in which he has been engaged for some time, to return to the farm. His address is Duntroon, Ont.

In renewing his subscription to the Review, Wm. Strong, of the class of '09, gives notice of his change of ad dress to Writing-on-Stone, Coutts, Al berta, where he is homesteading a quar ter section. He is among friends, there being several O. A. College ex-stu dents in the district in which he lives.

C. E. Craig, B.S.A., '03' writing from Lacombe, says—"My new address will be Aramalta, British Columbia. I am leaving here on the 15th inst. to man age a Fruit, Dairy and Poultry Farm, which is situated about three miles from Summerland, in the Okanagan Valley. The farm will amount to about sixty acres in all and for a start there will be five thousand trees, prin cipally peaches and apricots, to be set out." In renewing his subscription he says, "Everything in The Review in terests me greatly, even the locals."

H. A. Craig, Superintendent of Fairs and Institutes for Alberta, had charge of a two weeks' stock judging course held at Lacombe, several graduates of College being present. The course was a great success, and as is usual with such events, served to bring together several ex-students of College.

Beauty Wins.

Mr. Sydney Curzon, who was sent out by the family to prevent the mar riage of his younger brother Arthur, was completely won over to the side of the lovers by the beautiful bride and is now accompanying the young couple on their honeymoon trip as far as Los Angeles. The bride was Miss Evelyn Lethman of San Francisco, Cal., the wedding taking place in San Jose while on an automobile trip.

The Curzon brothers are graduates of the O. A. C., of the class of '94' and are better known to their classmates as "Sid and Tot."

Wm. Baillie, who came to Col lege in 1884, from Shooters' Hill, Mount Olivet, Jamaica, is at present at La combe, Alta. After graduation he went home to Jamaica, but soon re turned to Canada purchasing a farm a short distance from Guelph, where he resided until he went West. In the same district are several other old O. A. College boys. P. M. Ballantine, B. S. A., '07, has a splendid herd of Herefords. Geo. Stauffer, and Flack are homesteading near Stettler. Stauffer is still enjoying single blessedness, a condition of affairs that may be soon changed, however.

G. H. Hutton, B. S. A., '00, is manager of the Experimental Farm at Lacombe, and although he has been there but a short time he has accomplished a tremendous amount of good work.

T. B. R. Henderson, B. S. A., '04, Chief Weed Inspector for Alberta, is taking a trip east this spring. Rumor has it that he will not return alone.

We were favored, a short time ago, with a visit from W. Rush, B. S. A., '02, Rush is a market gardener, catering to Toronto trade. He has an excellent farm, and is handling it in a way that brings credit not only to himself but to his Alma Mater. The high esteem with which he is regarded by his fellow gardeners is evinced by the fact that he was once President of the Ontario Vegetable Growers' Association.

Henry Field went into the dry goods business in Cobourg immediately after graduation, and has made a success of it. He has served several terms in the town council and, last January, was elected Mayor. Field was always a wide-awake, energetic fellow, both at College and in business, and takes great interest in all things agricultural or horticultural.

E. B. Cutler, '96, was on the home farm at Birnam, in Lambton County, from the time he graduated until last spring, when he moved out West to Rouleau, South Saskatchewan. While in Ontario he was successfully engaged in dairying and swine raising—Holsteins, Ayrshires and Tamworths being his favorite breeds.

He was very fortunate with his crop last summer, harvesting 13,000 bushels from 420 acres. He is spending this winter in Ontario, and we expect that when he returns next spring he will not go alone. Although he likes the West, he is thoroughly alive to the advantages of life in Ontario, and anticipates returning at some future date to recommence farming in the Province of his birth.

Coldcotte, of '93, is travelling for an English firm.

W. A. Brown, '08, has just completed a very successful poultry short course at Orono, Maine, which was attended by our President. Brown is making good and has such a reputation throughout the State as a lecturer on Poultry, as to be in great demand for Farmers' Institute meetings.

Harry Dempsey, who took special work here some few years ago, is located at Trenton, Ont. He is Warden of Prince Edward County, and was a conspicuous figure at the opening of the new Collegiate Institute building at Picton.

Thomas Colgate, who was in the coal and wood business in Belleville, was also present at the Picton celebration. He has a good reputation as a vocalist and his songs were much appreciated.

The marriage of H. E. Taylor and Miss Nettie McLean, of Amherstburg, was quietly solemnized at the parsonage, Windsor, by the Rev. Mr. Manning. Mr. and Mrs. Taylor will spend a few days' honeymoon in Wayne County before taking up housekeeping in Gosfield South, where the groom has gone extensively into farming. Mr. Taylor is a graduate of the O. A. College, Guelph, and for some months assisted Mr. McKenney in the Agricultural Classes at Essex. He has a practical and scientific knowledge of agriculture and we predict that he will make good. Mr. and Mrs. Taylor are held in high esteem, and The Review wishes them every success in life.

W. A. Boutwell, an associate of the class of '09, is in the meat business in Barre, Mass. He has forsaken his single blessedness for the domestic bliss of wedded life, marrying Miss Ethel Harwood, of Barre. Since coming to Barre, Mr. Boutwell has won the esteem of his townsmen, and is one of the most popular young men in town. Both he and Miss Harwood were members of the Unitarian Church choir previous to their marriage.

OUR HERITAGE.

Not all the fire of Burns, the mind of Scott,
The stern and holy human zeal of Knox,
Nor that wise lore which human life unlocks
Of magic Shakespeare, Bacon's subtlest thought,
Nor Milton's lofty line sublimely wrought,
Not Gentle Wordsworth 'mid his field and flocks,
Nor Mystic Coleridge of the wizard locks,
Hath power to raise us to our loftiest lot;

But that rare quality, that national dream,
That lies beyond this genius at its core,
Which gave it vision, utterance; evermore,
It will be with us, as those stars that gleam,
Eternal, hid behind the lights of day,
A people's best, that may not pass away.
                              —Wilfrid Campbell.

Winter Mail Service in Prince Edward Island

BY T. C. JAMES, CHARLOTTETOWN.

PART II.

Despite the apparent hazardous nature of the crossing, comparatively few accidents have occurred, and these in almost every case might have been prevented had good judgment been exercised. In 1831 a boat with three men and a passenger was overtaken by a storm and forced to lie out all night. After suffering severely the men were rescued by a party from Cape Egmont P. E. I. In 1843 ten persons were out part of two days and a night, 36 hours in all. They suffered severely, some of them being badly frozen, but they finally reached the island shore. In 1855 three passengers with a crew of four men left Cape Tormentine for P. E. Island. When near the island shore a blinding snow storm set in, and they encountered the dreaded lolly. The boat was turned up on the ice for a shelter, and there, in a bitter frost, for two days and three nights, they suffered untold agony from cold and hunger. On the third day they killed and ate a dog belonging to one of the passengers, and revived by this food, after throwing out their trunks and other baggage, they struggled on toward the nearest shore, the coast of Nova Scotia. The start from New Brunswick was made on Friday morning, and on Monday evening one of the passengers, a Mr. Haszard, died. On Tuesday morning the survivors landed near Wallace, Nova Scotia, all badly frozen. The last accident happened in 1885. In January three boats with fifteen men and seven passengers started for New Brunswick under very unfavorable circumstances. A storm came on with blinding snowdrift. Towards evening they encountered lolly and drew up their boats on the ice. One of the boats was broken up, and with the wood and newspapers taken from the mail bags, they succeeded in making a fire. The relief obtained by the heat was more than counterbalanced by the effect of the smoke on their already in flamed eyes, and by the melting of the snow which saturated their clothing. The night was extremely cold, and next morning the drift was unabated. Toward afternoon they found them selves near the island shore, about fif teen miles east of the point from which they had started. After being thirty six hours on the ice, they succeeded in making their way to land, where they were very kindly treated. Most of them suffered severely from frozen

service at the Capes instead of the tri-weekly boats which hitherto had sufficed for the needs of the Province, and with making an effort to run a totally unsuitable wooden steamer be tween Georgetown, P. E. I. and Pictou, N. S. In the winter of 1876-77 a steam er, which had been built for ice service on the River St. Lawrence, was brought to P. E. Island, and the first real attempt made to solve the prob lem. This boat, the "Northern Light," in spite of many failures, due mainly to her construction, showed that much

CROSSING AT THE CAPES—CREW AND PASSENGERS DRAWING THE BOATS WITH STRAPS.

limbs which in some cases had to be wholly or partly amputated.

When, in 1873, Prince Edward Island annexed the other provinces of the Dominion to herself, one of the pro visions of the marriage bond was that the Dominion Government should maintain continuous steam service be tween the island and the mainland win ter and summer. This obligation, so far at least as the winter was con cerned, sat lightly upon the minds of the Cabinet. They contented them selves with establishing a daily iceboat

could be done, at least to improve con ditions. In 1889 the Government had the S. S. "Stanley" built in Scotland, specially for this service. The "Stan ley" is a ship of 914 tons gross, and of 300 nominal horse-power. Her success was marked, and in 1901 she was rein forced by a larger and more powerful steamer, the "Minto." By means of these boats navigation is kept up with very considerable regularity between Georgetown and Pictou, but in the view of Islanders the promise of Con federation has not been kept, and there are annual demands made by the Province Government upon the Dominion for the "pound of flesh nominated in the bond."

The worst stoppage in the history of these steamers occurred in 1903, when, the Stanley, in attempting to establish a new route from Summerside to Cape Tormentine, (a distance of about nineteen miles) was caught, January 12th, in an ice floe, and carried helplessly down the Strait, where she drifted, hopelessly imprisoned. Even dynamite

perience. So long as there is open water in sight they can generally make their way ahead. By means of water ballast the stern is depressed, and the bow thrown up so that when the steamer strikes heavy ice she runs upon it and breaks it down by her weight, long cracks running out in all directions. Often it is necessary to back in order to get headway and to charge again and again upon the mass before it parts. At times the boat wedges fast and can neither advance

THE S. S. STANLEY IN HEAVY ICE IN
NORTHUMBERLAND STRAITS.

failed to make any impression on the icy barrier which held her. The "Minto" in proceeding to her rescue, was jammed, and on February 28th, in an encounter with heavy ice, stripped every blade from her propeller. Both ships drifted up and down as the ice carried them, until, after an imprisonment of 64 days, the Stanley got clear, and with the disabled "Minto" in tow, succeeded in reaching port.

A trip on the winter steamers is to most people a novel and exciting ex

or retreat. Then all hands are ordered out on the ice, and with boat hooks, axes, etc., the ice is broken and pushed or pulled away till the steamer is freed and can steam ahead or astern once more. Field ice two feet thick is frequently handled without much difficulty, ice rafted cake upon cake to a height of from eight to fourteen feet is frequently encountered, but so long as west and northwest winds prevail passages can be effected with wonderful regularity. (The distance between

Georgetown and Pictou is about thirty five miles). When the wind sets in from the east and northwest the heavy ice becomes jammed between Pictou Island and the bight in which Pictou lies, and the nine mile passage becomes a solid mass. If this occurs with a high tide the ice masses, piled one upon another, are forced into shoal water, and at the ebb tide ground on the bottom. Then all hope of reaching Pictou must be abandoned until a southwest gale dislodges the barrier. It is doubtful if any ship can be built that will cope with these conditions, and in all probability continuous communication can never be kept up on this route. Various other lines have been suggested, each of which has its own advocates. It should be mentioned that both steamers are equipped with the Marconi Wireless Telegraph, and thus they are in continuous communication with the two shore stations at Cape Bear, P. E. I. and Pictou, N. S. The Dominion Government is now engaged in building a third steamer, larger and more powerful than either of those at present on the route. It is hoped that by this means much better results may be obtained. Meantime the Island's bill against the Dominion for breach of the Confederation contract is steadily mounting up, and if no redress is obtained the Treasury may find itself unable to meet the claim. A tunnel, costing anywhere from ten to twenty-five millions, is put forward by enthusiastic individuals as the only final settlement, but in face of a population of less than 100,000, and with little prospect of increase, the Dominion hesitates to incur such a large expense for the benefit of so few, the result of such a step being largely problematical. Meantime it is more than likely that for some years to come Prince Edward Island will be able to treat her winter visitors to the really delightful experience of a passage through our floating ice-fields in our staunch winter steamers.

A Winter Holiday in Cuba

In Cuba as in Canada a holiday falling on Monday or Saturday is doubly welcome. So in '08, while Cubans celebrated on February 24th, the opening of the Revolution of ——, we hailed the opportunity for a long talked of ride into the Trinidad Mountains, and a visit to the famous Hannabonilla Falls.

The prospective party diminished to six—all Canadians—with two Cuban guides and a boy in charge of the pack mule. Incidentally the latter soon earned the sobriquet of "Calamity Jane." Saturday evening saw us at a road-construction camp, about eighteen miles from Cienfuegos, where we were hospitably entertained by the American manager.

Having mastered the art of preventing starched and polished pillow-slips and sheets from skating about, on or off the narrow cots, we found it impossible to sleep because of the cold! Almost incredible to a Canadian, but even three heavy blankets would not prevent aching toes, with the mercury never below 46 degrees.

Five o'clock found us all astir in the grey of dawn, and after hot coffee, and our host's good wishes, we set out, the start enlivened by the unexpected bucking exhibition of one of the horses.

A few miles riding brought us to Cumaniyagua, a typical Cuban country town, with its fonda (hotel), thronged with idlers and dogs, its cafes, bake shop, tiny stores, and narrow, rocky streets swarming with goats, dogs, pigs, and children of all shades, be tween white and black, assuredly lur ing "the simple life," as regards cloth ing, at least. Some of the houses are of wood with red-tiled roofs, others are guama-thatched (palm-leaves), and still others of mud pressed into shape like cement. Having arranged for ac commodation here for the night, we pushed on; and a few miles more put us among the foothills.

Here the track became a bridle-path, past scattered tobacco farms, with their fields of deep green, and little clusters of thatched buildings. The hills be came steeper, small streams had to be forded in the valleys, stretches of woods intervened, and the farms were succeeded by pastures with herds of cattle and sheep. The increasing

height of the succession of cone-shaped hills lured us with the strongest fascin ation, and we pushed to the top, only to see a higher range across the valley, until the deep purple of the furthest mountains made a jagged line against the sky.

Some of the valleys broadened into a most pleasing prospect, of green fields and bright streams, beautified by the stately palm, or spreading umbrel la-like, agaroba.

Our guide enlivened the way by tales of some of the bloodless battles of the insurrections, as we crossed the sites, where twenty-odd thousand rounds of ammunition were fired.

Sometimes we were warned by jing ling bells to find a place and get our horses out of the track, while a train of loaded pack-mules passed on their way to the city.

At noon we halted to rest a little from the heat, at the home of a Span iard, who is trying his fortune at stock raising here. The house, on the peak of one of the cones, was of the cement like mud, with doors and casings of the beautiful Spanish cedar. The earth en floors contrasted sharply with the mahogany wardrobe and modern sew

ON THE ROAD TO CUMANIYAGUA.

APPROACH TO A SMALL FORD.

ing machine; and the immaculate starched muslins of the women and children were a marvel to the feminine half of the party. Mark the distinction between Spanish and Cuban! We were graciously entertained, the ever present black coffee served, and speeded on our way with good wishes, though one of the young ladies confided in us that centennes (gold pieces) at every turn would not tempt her to take the ride.

We pondered what life could be like, with the solemn hills on every side, and saddle and pack-mule the only means of transport to the city thirty five miles away.

Another hour and a half, with steeper climbs and narrower trails brought us in sight of the falls! A succession of five cascades, varying from ten to seventy feet in height—masses of foamy white, swallowed in the wonderful green of the deep pools below, the stream winding away between great cliffs clothed with limitless variety of foliage—palms, cacti with gorgeous bloom, orchids, ferns, and vines in wonderful profusion.

But it was eight hours since the early coffee, and even this scenery could not banish appetite, so all hands set to work unpacking provisions, or making fire, and preparing lunch. This over, two hours or more was spent in climbing, exploring, admiring, and making pictures, which after all do scant justice to the beauties of the scene. Repeated calls of our captain bring a reluctant party together.

Oh! for a week to camp in this ideal spot! But horses are saddled, and the homeward ride is more quietly taken, the mystery of the hills in the sunset light, with the deep purple of the valleys having a subduing effect upon all. But we need to hasten to reach the broader track before darkness falls—there is scarcely any twilight here—and eight o'clock found us again in the little town. The proverbial sauce, hunger, is a very necessary one to the enjoyment of a meal in that fonda.

For sheer drowsiness, we were scarce able to accept civilly the attention of our Spanish hostess, in whose house the ladies were to spend the night. Apologizing for the smallness of the room, she said that "if it were not very commodious, neither could it hold much cold." But this we were compelled to doubt before morning, despite our own extra blankets. The men, I believe, found tramping about preferable to attempting sleep, in the (apparent) zero weather of the fonda.

The Cuban custom of having coffee in bed, seemed to us very good the next morning, and the ministrations of our little hostess most grateful. Surely nowhere is exceeded the hospitality of these people.

A few hours more riding brought us again into the regular routine, with the determination. to revisit at our earliest opportunity, with equipment for a week's camping, the beautiful falls of the Hannabonilla.

L. W.

ONE OF THE SMALL CASCADES OF HANNABONILLA FALLS.

Among Ourselves

Winter Sports.

Although the season of winter sports has not been a favorable one for snow shoeing (always a favorite with our athletic girls) it has not proved dull in the sporting line. The excellent hills on all sides have been made very promising and beneficial use of as a scope for tobogganing, and judging by the rapturous reports of the partici pators snowshoeing will be but second to "bobbing" in future seasons. It is to be regretted that the hockey team, composed of such promising material, have had so little chance to show what they could do, and they are anxiously looking forward to spring and turf to renew their practices in ground hoc key. Snowshoeing and skating being so scarce the organization of a gymna sium has somewhat taken the place of out-door sport.

Y. W. C. A.

At the meeting on the evening of February 21st, Miss Katherine James read to the members present. The se lection chosen was taken from one of Margaret Sangster's book of talks. The topic was to the point and was of much interest to the listeners. A rare treat was enjoyed as well in the musi cal part of the meeting, as Mr. Fergu son, who was visiting the College was able to sing for us, and his song "O, Eyes That Are Weary," was very much enjoyed.

A reading by Miss Susie Tyson, en titled "Incompatability," was given at the meeting of the 28th of February, and was full of useful and practical suggestions. Miss Marion Rutherford accompanied the hymns.

The following Sabbath evening Mrs. Colonel MacCrea paid us a visit which as in the past was fruitful and pleasant. Her address was upon "Prayer," and her remarks, enforced by her pleasant and remarkable personality were appre ciated. Miss Alfreda Rogers and Miss Jean Flavelle accompanied the hymns, and rendered "Handel's Largo," very pleasingly.

"Woman's Opportunity," was the subject of a reading by Miss Blenner Hassett, on the evening of March 14th. The thoughts expressed were of an ap plicable nature, and much benefit was derived from them.

The Program Committee of the Y. W. C. A. has been much encouraged by the willingness of the students to take the meetings on several occasions, and they believe that the benefit has been mutual.

On the afternoon of the 26th of February, a sale of ice cream and sher bet was held in Macdonald Hall. The corridor of the second flat was cosily and prettily arranged as a reception room, and here the guests made them selves comfortable while enjoying the ice cream, etc., served by the white gowned young ladies. This sale being so successful another was held the fol lowing Friday evening, in the lower hall, which was also transformed into an attractive sitting-room. The pro ceeds netted the treasury of the Y. W. C. A. will materially increase their pros pects, and the members of the different committees in charge express their thanks for the enthusiastic support of the "Mac" girls.

The "Short Course" Promenade.

Last but not least of the many so cial gatherings at Macdonald Hall was the St. Patrick's Promenade, given by the Short Course, and whether or not they knew what St. Patrick—the Scotchman—did for Ireland, the stu dents of the O. A. College and Macdon ald Hall turned out in full force to cele brate his anniversary.

At half past seven the usual crowd of girls and boys were assembled in the main hall, discussing "How many" and "where?" Eight o'clock saw the pleasant task of filling promenade cards, completed, and with the announc ing of the first promenade the crowd dispersed to the upper halls, where cushioned seats were plentifully sup plied for the occasion.

Promenades were the order of the program with some exceptions, and the time allotted for these, was all too short. During the first promenade the college orchestra rendered "The So ciety Swing," and other selections, with their usual brilliant success. Mr. Howes favored the gathering with a selection from Drummond, and Mr. Lewis gave an amusing reading. The Misses Rogers and Flavelle delighted the audience with a violin duet, and the Misses Miller, Wylie, Walsh, Spence, Smellie and Mr. Lawson played during the remaining promen ades.

Refreshments consisting of ham and lettuce sandwiches and coffee were served at the west end of the main cor ridor. The tables were daintily decor ated with smilax and carnations.

The color scheme was green and white, and everywhere this was effec tively carried out. The reception com mittee wore white badges with green lettering. Everywhere the hall was decorated with large Shamrocks. The gymnasium was artistically arranged with Shamrocks and green ribbons. On the platform stood a venerable harp entwined with smilax, while green foli age was everywhere in profusion.

The most popular feature of the even ing was the gypsy tent on the main floor, where a palmist afforded great amusement for all those desiring to peep into the mysterious future.

The party broke up at the usual hour

and as the boys wended their way home their thoughts were probably more with the ones they had just left than with St. Patrick.

The work of decorating and arranging the hall was much lightened for the girls by the assistance of the Messrs. Moorhouse, Learmonth, Cutler, Lewis, Shaw, Kennedy and White.

A vote of thanks is due the members of the Short Course Class for their untiring efforts in planning the pleasant evening for the Long Course students during the strenuous preparation for the term examinations.

SUNSHINE AND SUNSHINE.

Much Ado About Nothing

The Bobbers.

Frances, Long, Mabel, Glad, Cassels
and Jean,
The greatest old bobbers that ever
were seen,
They fly down the hill at a terrible
pace,
And for safety, the steerer lies flat on
her face!

"I think I will steer," says Glad with a
grin,
"Now, girls, if you're ready, shove off,
we'll begin,"
Long sits at the back, and if dangers
should come
She's off in the ditch with the twist of
her thumb.

Jean knows she must balance, or else
there'll be strife,
While Frances and Cassels hang on for
dear life,

A yell comes from Mabel when half
down the hill,
"For goodness sake, girls, we're all go
ing to spill."

Zip! into the snowbank, they fly with
a dash
Bob, girls and snowdrift, great Scott!
what a hash,
Then up again, on again, off again—
they
Continue their bobbing the rest of the
day.

〜 〜

Miss F.—How do you make a sailor
collar?
Miss B.—Cut it from a three-sided
square.

〜 〜

Miss A. (sanitation class)—Another
form is when the gas is extracted, and
is called Coke.
Voice from the end of the room—Im
possible.

REPRESENTING ONTARIO, NOVA SCOTIA, SOUTH AFRICA,
NEW BRUNSWICK AND TEXAS.

In Ethics Class—Always discuss your principles even with your father, who may be older than you.

What is Massey?

To the public—A library.

To the students of O. A. C.—A ren dezvous.

Miss M.—Are you not worrying over skipping your class?

Mr. F.—It isn't the class, leave off the "C" and you'll find what's troubl ing me.

Miss M.—Leave off the "Cl" and you'll see what's worrying me.

Hints to Western Housekeepers by Some Who Know.

1. Do not sneeze or cough in the kit chen, for fear of disturbing those in the dining-room.

2. Always have the cold water chilly!

3. Be careful to look five or six times under the pillows to ensure yourself that you have left no ⅛-inch wrinkle in the sheet.

4. Never mind if you do use two dozen eggs trying to get six well poached. There are more hens at the O. A. C. dairy.

5. Never forget that there is a sure refuge for all badly cooked dishes!!

Miss P.—I heard about your coming up from town yesterday, and who did you walk with?

Miss B.—Indeed, I didn't walk with either of them, we girls walked in front and the boys behind.

Miss P.—My, but they must have been slow.

Miss B.—Oh, they had to be because they couldn't get past.

Homemaker—I can't turn this bread machine.

Miss G.—You'll have to get a man, then.

Inquisitive Freshman (commenting on the decorations at the St. Patrick's prom.)—Why don't you have a few four leafed ones hanging around?

Short Course Girl—Go to Professor Evans and ask him the difference be tween Shamrock and clover.

Miss B.—I wish I could wink to at tract attention.

Miss F.—Why don't you wiggle your ears instead?

Miss B- -y—I resemble a donkey in sound and name only.

Professor of English—What does it mean to drench a cow?

Miss—To wash it.

United We Fall:

Young lady to Diaz, Senior, at rink —Don't come near me or I will fall down.

~ ~

"French Translation."

Correct interpretation—We go into the shop to make some purchases.

Lewis's interpretation—We go into the shop to meet the employees.

~ ~

Professor—In whisky and water it is not a matter of equal quantities; what is it?

Hoffman—A matter of taste.

~ ~

Dr. Reed—There are some people who are so ignorant that they do not know in what year George Washington discovered the steam engine.

~ ~

Minister (closing chapel service)—Hymn two hundred and sixty-seven.

Baldwin (awakening from sleep)—Is it a kick?

Professor Day (Physics)—Is Mr. G. Young present?

Presant—He's out of the race.

Professor—What do you mean?

Presant—He's left the course.

~ ~

Student—Well, Reek, they have made you Professor of Physics, have they?

Voice from without—Don't you smell the gas? There's a leakage some where.

~ ~

S.—What does H. P. microscope mean?

J. P.—Horse power.

Swimming Feat.

WHOSE?

Professor D.—I have lost my notes on induction, or somebody has had the audacity to take them. I think it was in the year seventeen and fifty.

The Fancy Diver's Special.

Mr. Eastham—And what do we find inside the pericycle?

F.—The epicycle.

Professor—To get a natural distribution of trees, we might take as many stones as we have trees to plant, and throw them from us. Then plant a tree where each stone falls.

Peart—There's not much soil on the parlor floor.

⌒ ⌒

Thump, thump, thump, thump! (437 thumps per minute)

Bang! Bang!! R-r-r-ip!

Crash!. The building shakes, the windows rattle, doors are torn from their hinges, and everybody flees in terror.

The noise dies away in the distance like a rumble of thunder.

"What's the matter! Tornado? Messina earthquake? Bull get loose?"

No, gentle reader, be not alarmed. It was only Shaw going down to the telephone.

The Philosopher

of Metal Town

"Now, I'm not a professional builder, or a contractor, or a carpenter, but it seems to me I have had some building problem or other on my hands for many years—first, my own, then my boys', then my nephews', and my grand-boys'.

"Twenty-five years ago I became a pioneer user of metallic building materials.

"It was only a barn, and not much of a barn at that which I first covered with metallic shingles—the first product of the Metallic Roofing Co.

"And, mind you, that was twenty-five years ago, and the roof is weather-proof now. It has never needed repairs. I have built many barns since then, but I have never discovered any sane reason for roofing them differently. You can't improve on a straight 25-year test.

"Then besides, I always believe in dealing with the biggest people in any manufacturing business. You share in the merit of their goods which have made them the biggest in their line. That's why I stick to the Metallic Roofing Co.— they're the largest architectural sheet metal firm in Canada, with an output larger than all others combined.

"But it is not of barns alone I would speak. You note, perhaps, that they call me the 'philosopher of Metal Town.' That's because I'm a public character in a way.

"I have been chairman of many building committees—church, school, library, et cetera, and I always find the metallic man has been my most useful assistant. Outside or inside, front or back, ceiling or sides, I find they all need the metallic man's aid.

"I will tell you more about our 'metal town' when we're better acquainted. I can quote some comparative figures which will interest you. To-day I'm emphasizing shingles.

"You can get them either galvanized or painted. They are always reliable. They are more economically durable and quicker to apply than any others, fitting accurately, and therefore most easily laid. They have been thoroughly tested in all kinds of climates, invariably proving fire, lightning, rust and weather proof.

"If you're building, make sure of satisfaction by ordering Eastlake's for the roof. Fullest information if you write."

The EASTLAKE STEEL SHINGLES

The Metallic Roofing Co., Limited
Toronto and Winnipeg
Manufacturers for Metal Towns

Please mention the O. A. C. REVIEW when answering advertisements.

WINTER FEEDING OF DAIRY COWS.

The question of feeding should all hinge on the cost of production. The cows should, in theory, be made to produce their quantity, but in practice the cost of feeding must be kept down. In the ordinary way of feeding, the cost of making a cow that is doing fairly well give an extra quart of milk is very apt to be greater than the price realized for the extra quart. The reason is that the cow's digestive organs have been doing all they can do and extra feed is not only wasted to a great extent, but there is danger of throwing the cow off her feed. These difficulties may be completely overcome by feeding Herbageum regularly. In this way the maximum quantity of milk can be produced at the minimum cost and without the slightest danger from over-feeding. Herbageum is not a food. It simply aids in the digestion of food by supplying the aroma and flavors which are not in the dairy cow's winter food but which are necessary for thorough digestion and assimilation. A good substantial margin of profit may be made from the regular feeding of Herbageum to milch cows.

Prince Edward Island is a great dairy country, and we give below a letter from Mr. Benjamin Simmons, whose address is Charlottetown, P. E. I. At the Charlottetown Exhibition last year Mr. Simmons won first, second and third prizes on Grade Jersey and Ayrshire Cows. He writes as follows:

"I use Herbageum for cows and calves. I feed a teaspoonful to calves in each gallon of milk and when scarce of milk feed it in meals in about the same proportion. This keeps the calves growing and thrifty and prevents scours. To my cows I feed two teaspoonfuls to each cow. It makes an increase in the production of milk sufficient to show a good profit."

THE EXPENSE OF CONDIMENTS.

It is recognized by feeders generally that a condiment is necessary with stall feeding. A safe condiment must contain no dope of any kind. It must not be a tonic in a direct sense. It should act as a tonic indirectly by making the food more easily digested. It should not be expensive. Herbageum fills all the conditions. One fifty cent package is enough for one animal for eight months. It contains no drugs and it acts just as it should act. It is as natural and safe as a first class pasture. For cows coming in it is a great safeguard and for young calves it has no equal.

Shaw—Will you ask Miss —— to come to the 'phone, please?

Maid (who has just been resting after bringing the sixth young lady)—Which one do you want after Miss —?

～ ～

His teeth were standing on end, his eyes were chattering like a pair of cast anets, his hair was rolling down his cheeks in huge drops, and his mouth was as pale as new made cheese. As he spoke his limbs trembled in every nerve. Boys, I've swallowed a cockroach!

～ ～

Bill Ross (out tobogganing, finishing the journey on the seat of his trousers)—Aye! but it's good Scotch tweed, but I'm thinking there will soon be a sad, sad, parting, and the way is awfu' rough.

POINTERS
ON SOIL
FERTILITY

Amount of Manure Required

It is, of course, impossible to give any definite rules on this point, but tests conducted by Agricultural Colleges, Government Experts and others have proved that a light coating applied by a Manure Spreader gives much better results than a heavy application by hand; thus causing a given amount of manure to cover much more land and acre for acre the land will yield more with the smaller amount applied with the spreader.

Top Dressing of Field Crops

The Manure Spreader has made possible the top dressing of field crops which in a majority of cases gives the best results; for the first rain carries the fertilizing constitutents down into the soil directly to the roots of the plants, the top coating serves as a mulch to prevent drying out and also, in the case of fall sown crops, as a protection in winter.

Manuring a Meadow

This can be successfully accomplished by using a Massey-Harris Manure Spreader. It cannot be done satisfactorily by hand as the spreading would be very uneven and many large chunks would be left to find their way into the hay, rendering it almost, if not quite, unfit for use.

On Pasture Land

A light coating of manure can be applied with this Spreader so as to greatly improve the pasturage without causing the cattle to refuse to graze over it as would almost surely result from hand spreading. Many pastures which were almost worthless have been reclaimed in this way.

Massey-Harris
Co. Limited
Toronto
Canada

Professor Edward (has just asked a question)—Do you think Mr. Hutchinson is quite right?

A. W. Baker (who rooms with him)—No, sir!

∽ ∽

Cleverley to Smith—I notice you have stopped smoking.

W. H. S.—How's that?

Cleverley—You were home for Christmas.

∽ ∽

First Freshman—Say! The swimming conquest was pretty good, wasn't it?

Second ditto—Yes, but it wasn't as good as the boxing trurniquet.

∽ ∽

You see, boys, that each time I put in a bottle there is a greater effect. You can try this experiment for your selves, but be sure you use the Leyden jars, and not the flowing bowl.

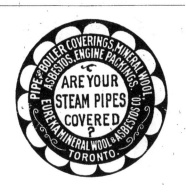

✍ IF YOU ✍

APPRECIATE

GOOD VALUES

You will be sure to buy your

SHIRTS, TIES, COLLARS, HATS
AND FURNISHING GOODS

Here. The choicest stock in the city.

My Tailoring Department is one of the most reliable in the trade. First-class, stylish clothing made to fit perfectly, and satisfaction always assured. See my stock of fine up-to-date goods. Only one price. Goods marked in plain figures. Be sure and give me a call

R. E. NELSON

Next Traders Bank.
Just above the Post Office.

Men's Furnishings
Hats and Fine Tailoring

First to show the New Fashions in Guelph--- MacDonalds'

For many years the leaders of fashions in Guelph, this store has always appealed strongly to practical women through the refined character of its styles and thoroughly serviceable quality of its goods.

Whether it is an outer garment or a piece of cloth you want, a bit of dress finery or a hat—whenever any need of the wardrobe develops, you will best satisfy that requirement by coming here.

Our customers KNOW that our styles are correct—that MacDonalds' Garments, Millinery and Fabrics are produced by the strictest observers of fashion; and our customers have reason to place equal confidence in our methods of selling—they know, also, that in this store they are offered the BEST of everything for the LEAST that can buy it.

D. E. MACDONALD & BROS.

GUELPH, ONTARIO, CANADA.

Oh, Freshman, you are charming.
Our poets long have sung
Their vilest verses to you,
And many times you're stung.
But none of us have ever
Told why it is, that you
Will always put your Christy on,
Ot dne gnorW.

The Dean (musing to himself)—"I wonder why all this sugar was put in the hall."

Voice from upper Hunt—"Frier pro tection."

∽ ∽

"All the great are dying and I'm not feeling well."—Willie Packard.

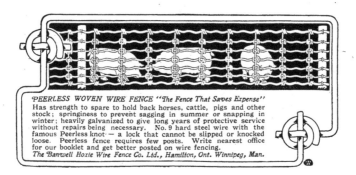

Those Bold Freshmen.

The Freshman class having made previous arrangements with the Manager, raided the Coliseum in a body, on February 15th. The management were completely taken by surprise, and no resistance was offered. A collection was taken up at the conclusion of the show.—Telegram.

~ ~

What Often Happens.

M.—"Say! I have a dandy joke for the locals, never heard anything as good before."

——"Let's have it!"

M.—"Gee! I've forgotten what it was!"

~ ~

Matsuda (at public speaking)—"The sugar beet is first shredded, then boiled from thirty to forty minutes, according to the size of the cook."

Please mention the O. A. C. REVIEW when answering advertisements.

CPSIA information can be obtained
at www.ICGtesting.com
Printed in the USA
BVHW050044061118
532207BV00022B/2419/P

9 780265 122198